ST

GET WHAT YOU PAY FOR

Other Books in the Need2Know Series

A full list of books can be obtained from
Need2Know, 1-2 Wainman Road, Woodston, Peterborough PE2 7BU

Help Yourself to a Job
Step by step into work
Jackie Lewis

Buying a House
Ease the path to your new front door
John Docker

Stretch your Money
Get more for your £££'s
Michael Herschell

Make the Most of Retirement
Live your new life to the full
Mike Mogano

Make the Most of Being a Carer
A practical guide to lightening the load
Ann Whitfield

Breaking Up
Live your new life to the full
Chris West

Successful Writing
The beginner's guide to selling your work
Teresa McCuaig

Superwoman
A practical guide for working mothers
Marion Jayawardene

Work for Yourself and Win
A practical guide to successful self-employment
Ian Gretton

The Expatriate Experience
A practical guide to successful relocation
Bobby Meyer

Forget the Fear of Food
A positive approach to healthy eating
Dr Christine Fenn Accredited Nutritionist

You and your Tenancy
A helpful guide to feeling at home
Sue Dyson

Improving your Lifestyle
Live a more satisfying life
Mike Mogano

Safe as Houses
Safety and security in the home
Gordon Wells

The World's Your Oyster
Education and training for adults
Polly Bird

Everything you Need2Know About Sex
The A-Z guide to increase your knowledge
Anne Johnson

Travel Without Tears
An essential guide to happy family holidays
Marion Jayawardene

Prime Time Mothers
A positive approach to delayed maternity
Lyn Cartner

Parenting Teenagers
Make the most of this unique relationship
Polly Bird

Planning Your Wedding
A step by step guide to the happy day
Niamh O'Kiersey

Make a Success of Family Life
A guide to getting along
Michael Herschell

The Facts About the Menopause
Coping before, during and after
Elliot Philipp

Coping With Bereavement
Julie Armstrong-Colton

Take a Career Break
Bringing up children without giving up Your Future
Astrid Stevens

Forthcoming books in the 1997 series

No Baby?
A Caring Guide To Subfertility,
Its Causes And Treatments
Dr Phyllis Mortimer

Help Your Child With Dyslexia And Other Learning Difficulties
Maria Chivers

Stress-Busting
The Essential Guide To Staying In Control
Nick Daws

Drugs
A Parent's Guide To The Facts
Judy Mackie

Education Matters
Help Your Child Get The Best From School
David Abbott

Winning At Relationships
The Ultimate Guide For Single People
Sheila O'Connor

Time For School
Get The Best Start For Your Child's School Days
Lyn Cartner

Beating PMS
Make A Real Difference To The Quality
Of Your Life
Sue Dyson

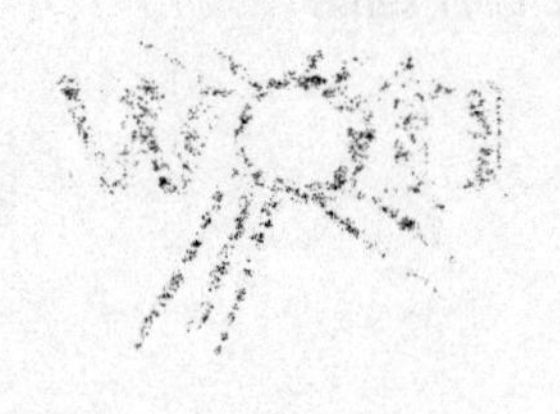

GET WHAT YOU PAY FOR

A Guide to Consumer Rights

Gordon Wells

Need2Know

ISBN 1 86144 023 5

First published by Need2Know, 1-2 Wainman Road,
Woodston, Peterborough, Cambridgeshire PE2 7BU
Tel 01733 390801 Fax 01733 230751

Edited by Kerrie Pateman
Design by Spencer Hart
Typesetting by Forward Press Ltd

Contents

Introduction

We hear a lot about consumer rights, but just who or what is a consumer? And what rights does a consumer have? A dictionary will tell you that to consume is to destroy, use up, eat or drink, spend or waste. But this gives a false impression.

Today, a consumer is anyone who purchases and uses goods or services. The emphasis is on the purchase, however paid for. The consumer is you, the ordinary shopper, the person in the street, the householder. And you want to get what you pay for.

Most of the time, we aren't that bothered about 'our rights'; we take them for granted - they're just 'there'. We go shopping; we buy something - clothes, 'hard goods', food, etc - we know what we're buying, we know what we're going to get for our money. We call in a plumber or consult a doctor or lawyer; we have a fair idea of the service we should get. Usually, we get what we expect: serviceable goods or competent service.

It's only when something goes wrong - the goods are faulty, the service is incompetent - that we start to wonder what we can do about it. That's when consumers' rights become important.

In this book, having outlined the law, we shall look at many areas where you, as the consumer, have rights; in each case, where relevant and appropriate, we shall:

- suggest what to do *before* you buy (or order a service) - as far as possible to avoid something going wrong with the purchase or service later.
- explain what you have a *right* to expect and how that right is safeguarded.
- investigate what you should do to rectify a fault - and suggest how and where to *complain*.

But there are other things in life than buying goods and services. We shall also look at how you pay for what you want - and how you are again protected. And, for part of your daily life you are perhaps employed: others are 'consuming' your services, for pay.

Here too, in the world of employment, you have rights which will be outlined.

And then there is the actual complaint process. This book will offer advice on the actual process: avoiding both shyness and aggression, and how best to complain - in person, in writing, in court. It will help you to... get what you pay for.

1

The Sale of Goods Act - Traders
The Supply of Goods and Services Act
The purchasing process

Most of us assume that if we take faulty goods back to the shop we bought them from, they will be replaced; that if we tell the plumber (or doctor) that their work has gone wrong, they'll put it right. In many cases that assumption is right... but it wasn't always thus, it might not be so elsewhere, and occasionally it won't be so here and now.

It is always possible that a less-than-scrupulous trader or service-provider will try to wriggle out of his/her responsibilities. Particularly if you don't know what you're entitled to.

Equally, to balance the above, traders will often make more allowances for consumers' foibles than they have to: many traders will allow the exchange of goods simply because the consumer belatedly decides that the size or colour of a purchase is not quite right. The trader is ensuring the consumer's goodwill.

The Sale of Goods Act

Nowadays, throughout the United Kingdom, consumers' rights are a matter of law. Note, though, that throughout this book it is English law only that, where necessary, is quoted. While the principles are nearly always much the same, there may be slight differences in Scottish law and its application. Check for yourself.

The Sale of Goods Act 1979 specifies that goods must be:

- of satisfactory quality
- fit for their purpose
- as described

Let's look at these points in more detail.

Quality

Satisfactory is a catch-all word that could mean different things to different people. The law says that goods must meet that standard that a reasonable person would regard as acceptable - bearing in mind the way they were described, what they cost, and any other relevant circumstances. They must also be free from all defects - even minor ones - unless they were sold as in that condition (crockery 'seconds' or 'shop-soiled' goods, for example).

You cannot expect a cheapo 'Made in Haiweiland' cup and saucer to be as fine - as smoothly finished, say - as expensive British-made crockery. But you can expect it to be properly glazed and free from chips and blemishes.

Suitability

To be *fit for its purpose* the same imported cup and saucer must of course, be non-porous... it must retain the liquid it holds. That's its purpose.

But fitness for a purpose means more than that: it also covers any purpose that you have told the seller about. If, for instance you tell a sales assistant that the kids want to play hopscotch on your drive and you want some paint to mark it out he must not sell you an indoor paint. If he does, you have a claim against the shop.

If you decide, unadvised, on the wrong kind of paint - having already mentioned its purpose - the assistant must warn you, before you complete the purchase, that the chosen paint will not be suitable. The fault or risk is then yours and the shop is not liable.

What it says

The *as described* requirement needs less explanation: if a pair of bedroom slippers is described without qualification as, say, fur-lined then the lining has to be real fur, not synthetic. The description - which can relate to quantity, composition, size, colour, or place and date of manufacture - may be on a display sign, an attached label, or on the carton in which the goods are packed. Or it may merely be what the shop assistant tells the shopper.

Traders

The provisions of the law, as explained above, apply to all goods bought from a trader: that is, a shop (whether a one-off store or a multi-shop chain), a street market stall, a mail-order business or a door-to-door salesman.

If you buy something privately - through a newspaper's classified advertisement columns, for instance - from someone like yourself, who is not a trader, you have fewer rights: these will be looked at in detail later in this chapter.

Whatever you buy though, no matter who from, the seller must have the right to sell it: that is, the seller must be the owner, or acting for the owner. The goods must not be stolen.

Safety regulations

There are also regulations about the safety of specific items. Such things as children's toys, clothing and furniture, many electrical goods, inflammable upholstered furniture, cosmetics, etc are controlled by strict safety regulations.

There are rules concerning the safety of food too. These are dealt with in detail in Chapter 2.

The Supply of Goods and Services Act

But consumers don't just buy things, they can also buy services: employ someone to do something for them. The person or firm providing the service could be a car repair garage, a plumber, a lawyer or a hairdresser. Any type of service is included. And once again, the consumer's entitlements are a matter of law.

The Supply of Goods and Services Act 1982 specifies that, unless more specific terms are agreed (see Chapter 5), a service should be undertaken:

- with reasonable care and skill
- within a reasonable time
- at a reasonable charge

Once again, let's look at these standards in more detail.

Care and skill

Like satisfactory (on previous page, Sale of Goods), the word reasonable needs to be explained. *Reasonable care and skill* depends on who you - knowingly - employ to work for you.

When you arrange for a job to be done for you, you have the right to expect a proper standard of workmanship. A repaired roof should not leak; a resurfaced drive should not peel off; a solicitor should not neglect any necessary part of your legal requirement.

If you employ an odd-job man to make you a dining room table though, and he takes the job on, while you can expect to get a serviceable table, you cannot expect it to be as well finished as if you had employed a furniture-maker. But if you employ a reputable firm of furniture makers, then you can reasonably expect the end product not to look as though it were made by an odd-job man. You should get what you pay for.

Any materials or goods - wood, bricks, fittings, spare

parts, replacement windows, etc - used in providing a service must comply with the terms of the Sale of Goods Act.

Reasonable care also includes looking after your property while it is in the care of the servicer. If you leave your car at a garage for servicing the garage must do its best to ensure that while in their care, it is not stolen or vandalised. Should such a disaster occur, the garage would have to demonstrate that they were not negligent in looking after it.

Time... and money

A *reasonable time* can be defined as the average time taken throughout the relevant trade or profession for doing a similar job. For instance, most garages could carry out an MOT test on your car in no more than half a day. If your garage started testing your car, then stopped halfway through while they worked on someone else's, so that you lost your car for three days, this is not reasonable. You could rightly claim compensation.

Similarly, unless a price has been agreed in advance, a *reasonable charge* is no more than about the average that others would charge for a similar job. It's always best to agree a price for a service before work starts.

It is not always possible though, for the provider of a service to know in advance what is entailed; they may not be able to tell you exactly what a job will cost. They should be able to give you an estimate though, which ought to be a good indication - as long as you both understand what the job is. But there is a difference between an estimate - which is at best an informed guess - and a quotation, which is a fixed cost agreed in advance.

The purchasing process

When you buy something - goods or services - you are reaching an agreement, making a contract with each other. That contract is enforceable in law. Once the contract has been entered into, you, the consumer have the rights spelled out above.

The agreement does not have to be in writing - nor even spoken; it can be implied. (If you fill your car with petrol at a priced pump, you have, by your actions, entered into a contract with the petrol station to buy an amount of petrol.)

In law, an agreement has to have:

- an offer by one person/party (eg petrol at 'x' pence per litre)
- an acceptance of that offer by another person/party (eg you've taken the petrol)
- a 'consideration', ie payment of some form (Note: under Scottish law, an agreement to do something for nothing is also legally binding).
- the intention of both parties to make a legal contract
- the legal capacity of each party to enter into a contract (The seller is entitled to sell.).

A trader may offer goods for sale - ie, offer to enter into an agreement - and seek to impose conditions on the sale; if these affect or reduce the customer's statutory rights they are not legal.

It is also important to understand that the contract is an agreement between you (the purchaser) and the trader (the seller); it is the responsibility of the trader, as seller, to give you your entitlement. It is not the responsibility of the manufacturer - no matter how much the trader may try to suggest this. And some will.

You do not need a bill or receipt as evidence of the

contract into which you and the trader have entered: think about an impulse buy of a packet of mints or a magazine at the aforementioned petrol station shop - you will seldom be offered a bill or receipt. If, after you have bought something, you need to make a complaint about it, documentary evidence of the contract is not necessary...but a sales or credit card slip will undoubtedly make the process quicker and easier.

It is most important that you save those little bits of paper - for a while, at least. Until you're sure everything's OK.

Something's gone wrong...

If the goods you buy or the service you have commissioned (and paid for) are not up to the proper standard, you, the consumer, have the right to compensation. You have the right to get what you pay for.

So...how do you go about it? The first thing is to tell the trader or service-provider that you are not satisfied. You have to complain. (But - see Chapter 10 - you should complain quietly and politely. Fine words butter more parsnips, they say.)

Most times, when you explain what is wrong, it will be put right, to your complete satisfaction. If not, there are further steps you can - and usually should - take. There are people who will help you - for some, it's their job. At the end of the day though, you may have to take a defaulting trader or service-provider to court. That's not so frightening as it first sounds though (more about this too, in Chapter 10).

2

Buying User Goods

Making the right choice - Descriptions
There's a hole in my bucket... - Buying bigger items
Agreeing price, delivery date etc - Buying a car

You are likely to be much concerned to *get what you pay for* - your consumer's rights - when you go shopping for specific personal, household, garden or leisure goods.

There are small purchases and big purchases. Once-or-twice-a-year items like clothes, toys, crockery, etc can reasonably be thought of as small purchases; new TV sets, computers, fridges, washing machines and the like, are big...and cars are clearly bigger. Houses are really big purchases. We need to be far more careful when making the bigger purchases than we do with the smaller ones. After all, it isn't the end of the world if a one-pound pair of socks isn't quite right. If you buy the wrong fridge-freezer though, you may have wasted several hundred pounds.

Before you buy

It's always wise to think long and hard before you buy

anything; certainly, anything major. Work through this pre-purchase check list:

- do you really need it? (Or is it an impulse buy, a move to keep up with the Jones family next door, or the result of advertising pressure?) This is probably the most important question of all - and you alone must decide the answer. The only source of help is to talk it through with a friend.
- is it the right one? (If you genuinely need a new or replacement...whatever, have you identified the most suitable and/or sensible make and model to meet your needs? For sources of 'outside' advice, see below.)
- will it do the job? (Are you buying something that does much more than you require? You may have to: things are becoming increasingly complex - the simple things may no longer be available.)
- is it the right size, shape and colour? (Take careful note - and measurements - before you decide.)
- if it's a replacement, is it genuinely better than what you already have? (Or does it merely look newer? Back to Square One: do you really need it?)
- must it be new, or would a good secondhand one be acceptable?
- is this the best price you can get? (In the post-Retail Price Maintenance world, you should always shop around for the best price. And there are often add-ons - such as extended guarantees - which may or may not be necessary and/or worthwhile.)
- can you afford it? (Cash or credit? There's more about financial matters in Chapter 7.)

Making the right choice

You have already decided that you definitely must have a new...whatever. The next most important thing is to make the right choice of make and model. And here, advice is often available.

Most public libraries have bound copies and up-to-date recent issues of the Consumer Association's magazine *Which*. Consult this for unbiased advice on best buys, best value for money, etc, on almost any item.

Many other magazines and newspapers offer occasional feature articles comparing various versions and models of similar goods: watch out for these when you are preparing to make a new purchase. And for some items - notably cars, hi-fi equipment and computers (PCs) - there are specialist magazines offering regular and on-going comparisons of available goods.

Checking on the price

Nowadays, few of us would be so foolish as to go into the first shop selling socks, washing machines, or whatever and make a purchase on the spot. We all know how sensible it is to shop around - for the best price, the best discount, the best terms. (Look out particularly, for shops advertising that they will match or beat any lower price in the area.)

When comparing prices, beware the 'extras'. High-pressure sales staff may try to persuade you, for example, to extend a 'standard' one-year guarantee for a further period. Look carefully at the cost of the guarantee extension. Guarantees are fine; extensions are not always worth investing in. Ordinary 'one-off' repair costs will frequently be less than the cost of the extended guarantee.

(An aside: I have a ball-pen with a - free - lifetime guarantee. That sounds great in the advertisements: it's a good selling point. It helped persuade me to buy the (excellent) pen. But of what value is the guarantee? What can go wrong? The actual writing part is replaced regularly; if the retraction spring breaks, any shopkeeper can replace it at near-zero cost. The guarantee costs the manufacturer virtually nothing - and I don't really need it.)

Investigate similarly the likelihood of something going wrongwith your purchase in its normal working life. It's better to avoid asking the sales staff - particularly the 'pushy' ones; try to find another user of similar equipment and ask about their experience. Most items of electronic equipment for instance will usually either develop a fault in the first few weeks after purchase, or not for several years.

Not only shops...

We can buy small, everyday items from a variety of places and traders:

- from a shop - whether that of an individual shopkeeper or of one of the big multi-outlet retailers.
- from a shop - at sale time ('Spring', 'Summer', 'mid-Season', 'New Year', 'Closing down', or any other excuse they can come up with to explain a sale).
- from a street (or regular fixed-market) market-trader.
- at an auction sale - new or second-hand.
- second-hand, through newspaper small advert columns, jumble sales, car boot sales, etc.

The consumer's rights are exactly the same when goods are bought from shops, or street/market traders and including those bought in sales.

New or second-hand?

Your rights are the same even when you are buying something second-hand - with the proviso that you cannot necessarily expect the same quality from second-hand goods as from new, nor if defects due to wear and tear were either obvious, or were pointed out to you before you paid for the item.

Consumer's rights are *not* the same though, when buying goods at an auction sale, or from private individuals.

At auction, you cannot back out of a purchase once the auctioneer's hammer has come down. Nor are auctioneers necessarily responsible for faults in the goods they are selling: there may well be specific clauses in their catalogues or posted on the saleroom walls.

If you buy something from a private individual - as a result of a newspaper advert perhaps - it has only to be 'as described'. It's up to you to satisfy yourself about the quality and suitability. *Caveat emptor* - let the buyer beware!

Covert traders

It is important therefore to make sure that the person you buy from in such cases is genuinely a private individual and not a trader pretending to be one. (Watch the local newspaper advert columns for the same telephone number appearing again and again, or for a seller who insists on coming to you, rather than you calling on him. Traders who sell through multiple small ads ought, by law, to make their trader status clear in each advert.)

If you buy anything of any consequence at a car boot sale it's usually fairly easy to differentiate between private individuals and traders. Individuals will seldom have more than one of anything to sell. It is always, though, sensible to make a note of the seller's car - make, model, colour and number - and to ask for a name and address. (Watch out too for counterfeit 'bargains' and for 'dodgy' - out-dated - food.)

It is against the law for a trader to pretend to be a private seller - doing so deprives you, the consumer, of your rights. Your local trading standards department will gladly take action against any 'covert trader'.

Exclusion clauses

You may occasionally - less often nowadays - see a sign in a shop saying 'No refunds given'. This is not legal: it is/was an attempt by the trader to escape his/her responsibilities. If you buysomething which turns out to be faulty, no notice can deprive you, the consumer, of your right to a refund. (Except at an auction.)

Descriptions

Your rights are further safeguarded in respect of what a trader may say about his goods.

We've all seen goods marked up in the shops as 'Sale Price ~~£15.99~~ £9.99' or 'Save £10 - Now only '£29.99'. These statements must be true; the goods must have previously been offered for sale at the higher price. If not, displaying such notices is a criminal offence.

There's a hole in my bucket...

As we have already suggested: most people are only interested in their rights when something goes wrong. And occasionally it will. What must you then do?

- You must, as soon as possible, take the purchased goods back to the shop, explain to the seller what is wrong with them, and state that you do not want them. You will probably find it wise to speak to someone at least one level above the original sales assistant - and be prepared to move up the management ladder if necessary. If you cannot quickly get back to the shop you should phone and advise them of your complaint. (And make a note of the time and date, what you said, who you spoke to, and their response.) You are entitled to 'a reasonable time' to examine the goods - at home.
- You do not have to accept a replacement item, a credit note or an offer of free repair. You are entitled to your money back. If you delay your complaint beyond 'a reasonable time' though, you may lose the right to a full cash refund - but you still retain the right to have the goods put right or the cost of a repair.
- You should not be fobbed off with the statement that the fault is the responsibility of the manufacturer - it isn't, it's the trader's. He must deal with it, and with you.
- If the item you have purchased would be difficult or expensive for you to take back to the shop ... you can, as long as it's within 'a reasonable time' again, ask the seller to collect it.
- You are not legally obliged to return faulty goods at your own expense. (This 'collect option' does not apply though to faulty goods which were given to you as a present from the actual purchaser. Indeed, with all such gifts, it is the actual purchaser who enters into the contract with the seller, has the consumer right in law ... and must therefore return them. But many shops will waive this requirement and deal with a complaint providing the gift-recipient has proof of the purchase - ie the receipt or sales slip.)

In many cases, complaints will be satisfactorily resolved in the shop when the faulty goods are brought back. If this is not the case, you will need to make a more formal complaint. There's more about how to complain in Chapter 10.

You have no grounds for complaint if:

- you actually examined the goods in the shop and could reasonably be expected to have seen the fault about which you are now complaining.
- your attention was specifically drawn to the defect but you still bought the goods.
- you are perhaps expecting too high a quality ... for the price you paid. (Basically, you get what you pay for.)
- you made a mistaken choice or have simply changed your mind and no longer like or want the goods.
- you caused the fault or damaged the goods yourself subsequent to leaving the shop.

...but even in those circumstances, many shops will still go out of their way to help you - by exchanging or repairing unsuitable goods. This is all part of their goodwill. (You're likely to buy from them again if they accommodate your foibles this time.)

Be careful though: credit notes - which are particularly appropriate in 'goodwill replacement' situations - are sometimes only valid for a limited period.

Buying bigger items

When you buy a pair of socks or a new kettle, you buy it and walk out with it. When you buy a bigger item - a double bed, a wardrobe, a fridge-freezer or a car - you may not walk out with it. The particular item you are buying may be either:

- too big for you to move and need to be delivered by the shop, or
- not in stock and/or have to be specially ordered (or even made) for you.

If the item is in stock but bulky, you should ask for agreement that you may pay for it on delivery (this may not be acceptable to the trader); more important, you should get specific advice - in writing, on the bill or receipt - of when the goods will be delivered. And this delivery should be within a few days.

If the item has to be obtained, once again, the delivery date should be determined - and specified in writing. You may well be required to pay a deposit when ordering the goods. Take care: while it is reasonable to pay a deposit to a reputable and established shop, you should think twice before paying a deposit to a trader you know little about, operating perhaps from a post office box.

If you pay a deposit and the seller ceases trading, you are likely to lose your deposit. Equally, with any business, if you cancel your order after paying a deposit, you can forfeit the deposit. Remember: once you have agreed to buy something, a contract exists even if the goods are not yet in your possession.

Delivery dates

If you agree a delivery date and the supplier fails to deliver on time, then the supplier has not fulfulled his part of the contract. You are entitled to ask for your money back. If no specific delivery date is agreed, the supplier can be expected to deliver within 'a reasonable time'; this is usually interpreted as within 28 days.

Alternatively, if you have not agreed a delivery date when ordering goods - and the delivery is dragging on and on (say two or three months) - you can write to the trader saying that now, *time is of the essence* (use those words) and set them a reasonable deadline for delivery. A further fourteen or twenty-eight days would not now be unreasonable. Tell the shop that, if they fail to meet the new deadline, you want your money (or deposit) back.

Once you have specified an extended delivery date though, you cannot, during that period, cancel the sale.

Agreeing a price

When buying for later delivery you should, whenever possible, agree the price with the seller - and have it recorded on the bill/invoice/receipt. In this way, you may be able to ensure that, even if the manufacturer's price rises before delivery, you don't have to meet that increase; alternatively, you may be asked to agree that you *will* pay such increases. It can be a matter for negotiation between you and the seller. (If there is an increase in VAT (Value Added Tax) before delivery of an ordered item though, you will have to pay this excess.)

Maybe the item you are buying is not in the catalogue - perhaps you are asking for a variation in the norm - or the catalogue makes clear that prices are subject to variation, and the trader doesn't know how much the manufacturer will charge for this variation; you should seek to agree on an estimated 'ball-park' cost - or an upper limit. The important thing is to get it straight ... and preferably in writing.

On delivery

When goods are actually delivered, you may be asked to sign a note of acceptance. It is wise to annotate any such signature as 'goods received - unexamined'. You are entitled to 'a reasonable time' to examine whatever you buy.

As with smaller items, if you keep goods, without complaint, beyond a reasonable time, you are deemed to have 'accepted' them. Once 'accepted', you lose your right to reject them.

So...once an item is delivered, you should examine it carefully and try it out: if it is in any way faulty, notify the supplier quickly and your rights are safeguarded. And remember, you do not have to arrange for it to be taken back to the shop: the supplier has to collect it.

Buying a car

A (new-to-you) car is one of the biggest single investments many of us make. It is therefore wise to be particularly careful. Points to consider include:

- Take account of all the costs - running costs (petrol, etc), insurance, road tax, MOT, maintenance (and repairs) ... and the cost of credit - when deciding how much you can afford.
- Check in (up-to-date) car magazines for reviews of your chosen car - and its competitors; check 'standard' trade-in value of your present car.
- Look around for discounts: it is seldom necessary to pay the full advertised price for a new (or second-hand) car. Check on trade-in allowances offered - and compare them with the discount if you pay all cash (by selling your present car privately). Watch out for 'cash-back' offers too: these are sometimes a means of avoiding giving a formal discount.
- Be prepared to haggle with the car dealer - even on the cost of credit. It is usually best to let the dealer make the first offer - of trade-in, discount and overall package price, etc - so that you have a base to negotiate from.
- Don't be afraid of walking away from a possible deal - you should always take time to think. Ensure that you understand all that's contained in any 'package'.

- If buying a second-hand car from a dealer: investigate the mileage reading (the clock can be turned back - even though it's illegal); get a knowledgeable person (eg someone from the AA or RAC) to help you check the car's condition; ask to see the last MOT certificate, the vehicle registration document (the log book) and unless it's old, the car's service record book - enquire generally about the car's recent history, and check the ownership. If the dealer is reluctant to answer any reasonable questions about the car it's often wisest to walk away.
- Take a test drive - first making sure that your own insurance covers you for this. Perhaps get the aforementioned knowledgeable person to test drive the car for you as well as yourself.
- If buying privately - ie from someone other than a trader - make all the above checks but also remember that you have fewer consumer rights and the seller does not have the overhead expenses of a dealer: the price agreed for a private sale should be less than from a dealer.

Remember: a car is a major investment. Be careful.

3

Labels - Additives - Eating out
There's a fly in my soup... - Ho-o-o-ow much?

While 'user' goods - clothes, fridges, TV sets and cars - are costly, they are only occasional purchases. Even the most expendable items are seldom replaced more frequently than every few months and sometimes, as with a new car, at several-year intervals. Things to eat though, need to be purchased afresh all the time; it's an ongoing process. Few items of food will keep, unprotected or untreated, for many days. Most of us, from time to time, buy our food either:

- for home preparation and consumption - ie the daily/weekly shopping basket; or
- cooked by someone else and served to us, in a restaurant.

The Law

In both situations, our rights as consumers are protected. The law does its best to ensure that we are neither harmed nor cheated. It is against the law (the Food Safety Act 1990) to supply food which is unfit for human consumption and/or injurious to health; it is also an offence to describe, in a false or misleading way, the nature, quality or substance of food. There are strict rules too, about the way food is prepared for sale or consumption - these are enforced by local government environmental health officers. Restaurant kitchens and food preparation areas are inspected regularly.

At the same time, and overlapping, any food sold must comply with the basic requirements of the already-mentioned Sale of Goods Act 1979; food items must be of a satisfactory quality, fit for their purpose, and as described.

Labels

One important way to make sure that you get what you pay for when doing the weekly shopping is by paying attention to the labels on packaged foods. The law ensures that the labels do not give false or misleading descriptions. They also tell us whether the food is stale or still safe to eat. The labels are particularly useful in checking on value for money and the ingredients used in preparing the food - there may be some things you don't wish to eat. Specifically, food labels give information on:

- the ingredients (including additives - see page 36) used in preparing the food, listed in decreasing order of weight (ie, the biggest ingredient first) at the time of their use in the preparation of the food.

  This information allows consumers to avoid ingredients which they don't want or shouldn't eat. It is also particularly useful in checking value for money - if tomatoes are low on the list of ingredients in a tin of tomato soup, this could indicate a poor quality soup.
- the quantities of any ingredients that are specifically identified in the product description.

For example, if a product is described as 'low fat', then the proportion or quantity of fat should be shown on the label - and it should be significantly lower than in the usual version of the product. This statistical information is often included in the listing of ingredients.

- the date by which the product should be consumed.

  This may be: a 'use by' date which is usually applied to highly perishable foods - it does not necessarily mean 'eat by' but may also be interpreted as meaning 'cook by' - and is a date beyond which the food, as is, will be a health hazard; or a 'best before' date which does not mean that thereafter the food becomes a health hazard, but that it will no longer be at its best. The datemark doesn't have to be on the label but it must be prominently displayed and the label must say where to look for it - on bottle-cap or can-base, for example.)

- how and where, and for how long, the food should be stored.

  For example: 'Once opened, store in refrigerator; use within one month of opening.'

- nutritional value.

  This is only a legal requirement if a specific claim is made elsewhere on the label - see above; it is though, increasingly provided, irrespective of any claims. Where provided, the nutritional values must be tabulated in quantities (calories [kcal] and kilojoules [kJ], or grams [g]) per 100g or 100ml - it is also often given as per serving or pack - against such items as energy, protein, carbohydrate, fat, fibre, sugars, sodium (salt), etc. The figures are useful in matching individual dietary requirements.)

- the name and address of the maker, packer or retailer, so that any complaint can be accurately targeted.

- the content of the pack - and nowadays, this will be in metric units.

  A large lower-case e alongside the content figure means that while the weight of individual packs may vary slightly, the average per pack is accurate.

Pay particular attention too to the precise wording used in describing items of food. An *orange flavoured* product must actually get its flavour from real oranges; an *orange flavour* (ie without the -ed) product merely tastes orangey... but need have no real orange content. Similarly, bacon flavour potato crisps are strictly vegetarian, having no bacon content at all.

Additives

Many people are concerned about the additives used in food preparation. But without additives some of our food would look quite different and in some cases would not keep as well as we expect it to.

Both the British government and the EU test additives for safety. Some additives are natural, such as beetroot juice (E162); some are man-made versions of a natural product, such as potassium nitrate (E252); some are man-made and not in nature, such as saccharin (un-numbered). All are tested; nearly all are given approval numbers by the British government; many are also tested by the EU, in which case an E is added to the approval number.

Some commonly-met additives with their numbers, full names and uses are:

E320 butylated hydroxyanisole (BHA): an antioxidant used to stop fats and other substances in some foods - soup mixes, cheese spreads, etc - from combining with oxygen and going rancid.

E150 caramel: a colouring, used to maintain or brighten the natural colour in beers, soft drinks, gravy browning, etc.

E322 lecithins: an emulsifier and stabiliser used to mix oil or fat with water and prevent later separation - used in low fat spreads and chocolate.

E249 to E252 sodium and potassium nitrites and nitrates: preservatives which have been in use for centuries, which also give the distinctive pink colour in bacon, ham, corned beef, etc.

621 monosodium glutamate (MSG): a *flavour enhancer* (Has been accused of causing bad reactions but scientific tests have failed to prove this.)

aspartame: an (un-numbered) artificial low-calorie sweetener used in soft drinks, etc.

If you want to know more about the additives used in your food, and a list of all those approved, the Ministry of Agriculture, Fisheries and Food publish a free booklet, explaining the purpose, importance, testing and safety of additives: Tel 0645 556000 or write to Foodsense, London SE99 7TT for a copy of Foodsense booklet number 2, about food additives (PB0552).

What to do

When choosing foodstuffs you, the consumer, can decide what to buy and ensure that you get what you pay for by consulting the product label. The label will also help you determine the 'best buy' as you shop around, which is always wise. And the regular checks and inspections will, in most cases, ensure that your food is safe.

If you do find something wrong with the quality or condition of the food you buy though - whether packaged or not - you should take it back to the shop that sold it to you. They will usually be able to satisfy you. If not, contact your local authority environmental health department. They will arrange for the food to be tested and if appropriate, will prosecute the shop and/or manufacturer.

That prosecution won't get you your money back... but if it is successful, you can use the court's decision to claim compensation for any loss you have suffered. And you can at least feel good that others will not have to suffer from the same fault.

If you buy food 'loose' - ie unpackaged, weighed for you by a shop/trader - and believe that you have been given short measure and/or overcharged, complain first to the trader. In most cases, if correct, you will gain compensation and be satisfied. (If proven wrong...you'll get 'egg on your face', but avoiding short measure is worth occasional embarrassment.)

If you are still concerned, and believe the short measure was not accidental, you may wish to make a formal complaint - in this case to the weights and measures section of the local trading standards department. The trading standards inspectors are also the right people to investigate complaints about inaccurate labelling of food products.

Eating out

From time to time most of us eat out, in pubs or restaurants. And often, even if there is something wrong with the meal or the service, we don't like to complain... because we don't want to spoil the occasion. This attitude is wrong; most times the fault can and will be rectified by an apologetic management.

First though, it is wise, as always, to survey the choice of places at which to eat out. Listen to the recommendations of reliable friends; note the restaurant reviews in local newspapers and magazines... and add a pinch of salt. (Some reviewers praise unselectively in exchange for hospitality.)

Where possible, in advance, look at the menu (and prices, if indicated) displayed outside a restaurant of choice, or on the pub wall. Be sure that you can afford the prices... and all the extras. Does it look as though you'll get what you pay for?

Make your choice of venue. It may be necessary to book a table. Think carefully before doing so, because once you and the restaurant have agreed a booking by phone, you have entered into a contract. The restaurant would be within its rights to seek payment - for blocked table-space if nothing else - if you fail to turn up.

What's on the menu?

You arrive at your chosen restaurant on time - or on spec - are ushered to a table and presented with the menu. Now is the time to complain if your table is next to the toilets or the kitchen service door - don't wait until the meal is being served, to ask for a move.

Once seated, you should not have to wait too long before someone comes to take your order: five minutes is reasonable.

When studying the menu, note what is included in the price for each dish, or which courses are included in a fixed price menu. (If, for instance, coffee is not included in a fixed menu, take note of what it will cost: maybe you could do without and go home for coffee.) Take note of whether a service charge is automatically included - you wouldn't be the first person to unwittingly add a sizeable tip to an already generous service charge.

And order your meal.

How long you should have to wait for the meal itself to arrive is a matter of judgement: some dishes will take longer to prepare and serve than others - you must make allowances.

You have the right to expect that:

- your meal will be of satisfactory quality (commensurate with its price - that is, you should get what you pay for)
- the dishes (and wine) will be 'as described'
- the food will be served hot (or cold, if appropriate) and the wine too, served at the correct temperature

- the meal will be served on clean, unchipped plates with clean cutlery and un-smeared glassware
- the service will be satisfactory (and, you hope - cheerful).

There's a fly in my soup...

If there is something wrong with the food you should complain as soon as possible. It is unreasonable to wait until the end of the meal and then complain: that smacks of an attempt to reduce or avoid payment. Explain - quietly - to the waiter what you feel is wrong with the particular dish. Ask for the manager if the waiter is unhelpful. In most cases the restaurant will be happy to make amends: they might offer an alternative from the menu, or remove the sub-standard dish and rectify the fault.

(A friend, dining at a famous London restaurant, discovered a live caterpillar in a side-salad; he complained, showing the intruder to the *mâitre d'hôtel*... who declared it 'impossible'. Within seconds, the table was surrounded, stripped to the woodwork, and relaid; the whole meal was replaced. At the end of the meal there was no bill - just apologies. It is right to complain: a good restaurant has a reputation to uphold and would want to know of mistakes.)

If the service you get is not up to expectations, you should similarly make plain your dissatisfaction during the meal.

Ho-o-o-ow much?

Whether or not you have a complaint, you should always check the bill carefully. Errors are not uncommon.

And finally, if at the end of the meal you remain

dissatisfied with either food or service and have already made this clear, you can, when presented with the bill, offer to pay what you think is a reasonable amount instead of the full sum. You must then, if asked, give the manager your name and address.

If the food has been good but the service poor, you are within your rights, if a service charge is included, to deduct some or all of this to reflect the quality of the service you feel you received.

Usually, when actually confronted in this fashion, the restaurant will accept the situation and not attempt to sue you for the amount(s) deducted - but you must be prepared for this outcome. (If you have complained - calmly and with reason - throughout the meal, you will usually win.)

If the restaurateur calls the police, wait for them to arrive, explain that you have complained throughout the meal and that you are not avoiding payment, merely exercising your right to deduct a reasonable amount from it. As long as there is no breach of the peace, the police have no grounds to intervene.

If you wish to avoid this degree of confrontation though, you can pay the full bill and then, later, take the restaurant to the Small Claims Court (see Chapter 10) for payment of the difference between what you paid and what you think would have been a reasonable amount.

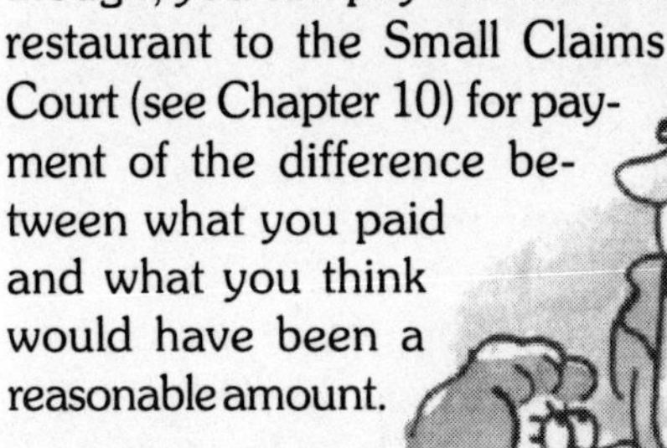

But...chances are you won't bother.

4

The law - and more - Sensible mail order procedure
Mailing lists - Faulty advertisements - Credit card buying

Increasingly, we are buying user goods from the comfort of our own home - by post or phone. There have long been advertisements in newspapers and magazines for some mail-order goods; nowadays there are many more. Lavishly illustrated catalogues too arrive regularly by post, seductively urging us to order the goods so beautifully portrayed therein. And, without doubt, they are tempting.

The law - and more

You have the same consumer's rights when you buy goods by mail order or by phone as you do when buying from any other trader; goods must be of satisfactory quality, fit for their purpose, and 'as described'.

You may have even more rights when buying by mail order: the Mail Order Traders' Association (MOTA) requires a high standard of consumer protection of its members. Most reputable mail-order companies allow customers to return goods within a specified number of days (usually one or two weeks)... simply because they don't like the item.

If you buy something in response to a newspaper or magazine advertisement you often have further protection. Publications that subscribe to the Mail Order Protection Scheme (MOPS) ensure that their readers do not lose their money if the advertiser ceases trading. (The scheme does not apply though, to advertisers selling perishable food or medical products, or within the publication's classified advert columns.)

We have already explained that when you buy something you are entering into a contract with the seller. When buying by mail order the contract is made when the seller posts - rather than when you receive - a letter confirmating receipt of order, or the goods themselves.

Sensible mail order procedure

As with any other purchase, when buying by mail order, whether from a mail-order catalogue or in response to an advertisement:

- think first:
  - do you really want/need this item? (Or have you been 'carried away' by the picture?)
  - can you get the same thing cheaper elsewhere? (When comparing, don't forget the post and packing charge which has to be added - check whether it is a fixed charge for any number of items or a charge per item.)
  - can you afford it? (You may buy 'essentials' on credit; many mail order goods are 'wants' though, rather than 'needs'.)
- read the rules, the 'small print':
  - will you be dealing with a reputable/established firm?

- can you return the goods without paying for postage, etc?
- is a delivery time specified? (28 days should be a maximum)
- for how long is the catalogue price valid? Can the firm increase the price without your agreement?

☼ decide whether to order by phone, fax or post:
- if ordering by phone/fax remember that you will need to use a credit card (which may be advantageous, see below) - have it handy when you phone
- phone or fax may bring quicker delivery
- if by post, do not send cash: pay by cheque or postal order, retaining a fully-filled-in stub in either case... or pay by credit card
- make a note of the date of a phone order, and ideally, the name of the person to whom you spoke

☼ retain the advertisement or catalogue until you have received the goods you've ordered. (If the advertisement was in a magazine or newspaper that you don't take regularly, keep the whole publication for the date, its address, etc, in case something goes wrong.)

☼ when the goods arrive, sign any delivery note as 'unchecked' or 'not examined' - then once opened, check them as quickly as possible; as far as possible keep the packing materialintact and reusable until you are satisfied with what you've got.

☼ if there is a fault - or even if you just don't like what you've got - it's often wise to phone the mail-order firm's Customer Service Department. (Check the 'small print': the firm may insist on such a phone call before any goods are returned.) Whether or not you phone in advance, you should return the faulty goods as soon as possible, preferably in their original packing, accompanied by a note detailing your complaint.

☼ most times, any fault, complaint, or report of un-received goods will be dealt with quickly and courteously - mail-order firms need your goodwill. Only if you fail to get satisfaction will you need to take the matter further. You can write to the advertising manager of the publication in which an advertisement appeared and seek redress; if still dissatisfied, you can contact the MOTA. (Address in Help List.)

I didn't order that!

Occasionally - and now rarely - a 'pushy' mail-order firm may send you unsolicited goods, goods that you haven't ordered, in the hope that once seen, you will decide to buy them. This sales technique is now regulated by the Unsolicited Goods and Services Act 1971.

If you receive unsolicited goods, write to the seller giving your name and address and stating that you have received...(whatever), that you didn't order it and don't want it, and giving the seller thirty days in which to collect it from you. Keep a copy of your letter. If they then don't collect within the thirty days...the unsolicited goods are yours, free.

If you can't even be bothered to write, put the goods aside, unused. Providing that you do not subsequently agree to accept or return the goods yourself, and if the supplier does not collect them within six months... again, they are yours, without payment.

It is illegal for the supplier to demand payment for unsolicited goods. But nowadays this is an uncommon sales technique: don't hold your breath waiting for an unsolicited and 'soon-to-be-free' sports car or cocktail cabinet.

Book and record clubs

We've all seen the lavish advertisements, often in weekend newspaper supplements, for book and record clubs. The offers always look attractive: 'Choose five books (or CDs) for £1 - plus post and packing.' (And the 'plus p & p' qualification is sometimes only in small print on the application form.)

Without doubt, book and record clubs offer good value for the money you spend - and the 'start-up' offers are marvellous value - but you should always think before you sign up. Ask yourself:

- Do I really want the books/CDs I'm getting or am I just ordering them because they're so cheap? (Everyone loves a bargain.)
- Are the start-up offers as good as they appear? (Add in the post and packing charge before you decide.)
- Are the start-up offers returnable - if you don't like what you get, can you return them and cancel the whole membership? (Most clubs allow you a couple of weeks inspection before the membership becomes a contract. If you do decide to return your start-up offer, it is wise to post them by recorded delivery, or at least get a certificate of posting from the Post Office.)
- To what are you committing yourself, beyond the start-up offer? (You will usually have to buy a book/CD per month for the next several months before you can cancel your club membership. Most clubs let you reject the month's 'star' book or CD and select an alternative from their list; the best permit you to reject the star offer... and all others too. As long as you write back quickly each month, you may not have to buy any book or CD beyond the start-up offer. But you should check carefully.)
- Of what quality are the books/CDs supplied by the club? (Nowadays they're usually excellent, but I recall belonging to one book club many years ago whose admittedly inexpensive monthly books were poorly produced.)

If you have reason to complain about the goods you receive from a book or record club, write to the company first; if you get no satisfaction you can approach the Association of Mail Order Publishers (For address see Help List.) They do not offer an arbitration service as such but may be able to help. If the club advertised in a magazine or newspaper and has subsequently ceased trading, you may be able to get your money back through the MOPS system already mentioned.

Mailing lists

The names and addresses of people who buy (or have bought) goods by mail order are valuable information. Some mail order firms permit other firms the use of their mailing list. As a result, you may be inundated with catalogues from firms with whom you have never done business. Some of us don't object to this 'puff mail' - all we have to do is bin the inappropriate catalogues and glance through the interesting ones. (It just takes will-power not to dash off and order.)

There are two ways of avoiding 'puff mail'.

When next you respond to an advertisement or mail order catalogue look for the tiny opt-out box. One form on my desk as I write says, in tiny print, 'From time to time we may make our mailing list available to carefully chosen companies whose products or services might interest you. Please tick this box if you do not wish to receive such offers.' If you don't look carefully you could easily miss this... as do most people. If you don't want even more 'puff mail', tick the box.

The alternative way to stop most (?) 'puff mail' is to write to the Mailing Preference Service (address in Help List) and ask for your name to be deleted from all mailing lists. This will work, given time: allow three months.

You may wonder how all these firms can afford to send out catalogues and special offers that most of us just throw away. Clearly it must pay off, or they'd go out of business: apparently, they only need a 2 per cent response for financial viability.

Faulty advertisements

If you believe that any goods you have ordered from

an advertisement were misrepresented in the advertisement, you should report this to the Advertising Standards Authority. They will investigate your complaint. They won't order the culprit to make compensation, nor will they take legal action on your behalf - but they will make sure that others are not similarly swindled. The Advertising Standards Authority is a powerful and influential body in its own right though, so you may find that you get your compensation from the defaulting trader anyway.

Credit card buying

There are potential advantages in buying goods by credit card.

If you buy something costing more than £100 (and less than £30,000 - seldom a major consideration) using your credit card and the goods are faulty, you can claim compensation from the credit card company. The Consumer Credit Act of 1974 makes the credit card company jointly liable for any claim you may have against the trader. This is particularly relevant if the trader ceases trading. It is best to approach the trader first - and the credit card company will often press you to do so. But you don't have to.

Note too that this added protection applies only to credit cards, which permit you to spread payment over time: it does not apply to debit cards, where payment is taken from your bank account immediately. Nor does it apply to charge cards, where you have to pay all you owe within a specified period.

It's worth thinking about this added protection - particularly when buying things like personal computers or package holidays.

5

Quotation or estimate - The goods
They're not doing the job properly - Contracts
Off on your hols

We don't only buy goods: at some time or another, we all employ someone else to work for us. We buy their services.

The services we buy can range from a haircut to a new roof on our home, from a dental filling to a will, from refuse collection to water on tap. Your rights - to get what you pay for - are much the same across the whole range of services... but the ways to ensure them may vary.

So... in the next three chapters we shall look, separately, at everyday private sector services, professional services and public services. First - private sector services.

Private sector services range from the simplest everyday tasks to the most sophisticated; from people or firms who will cut your hair, clean your clothes or service your car, to those who will redecorate your house or take you on holiday. And all stations in between.

We have already, in Chapter 1, outlined the consumer's legal rights in respect of services: that the service must be provided with reasonable care and skill, within a reasonable time, and, if a price has not been agreed in advance, for a reasonable charge.

Check first

Before commissioning a service though, the wise consumer will:

- enquire from other service-users about who has a good reputation as a plumber, hairdresser, etc. Are your neighbours satisfied with their new drive, kitchen or carpet?
- enquire the likely price from more than one relevant service-provider - and before you commission the work, get a firm quotation...in writing.

Word-of-mouth recommendation by satisfied customers is by far the best guarantee of a good job. And of course, once you've found yourself a reliable plumber, electrician, decorator, odd-job person, etc - keep a careful note of their name, address and phone number. 'A good man these days is hard to find.'

If you fail to investigate the likely cost of a job before you commission it... you can hardly complain if it costs more than you expected. (Only if the bill is 'unreasonable'.) Anyway - you need to be sure you can afford it.

Quotation or estimate

There is an important difference between a quotation (or 'quote') and an estimate. You ask an electrician, say, to give you a price for fitting a new power socket in your kitchen. The electrician knows how long it will take to do the job and the price of the fitment. 'I charge £25 plus VAT for a new power point,' he says. That is a quotation; the price is fixed - except for the VAT. (If the Chancellor of the Exchequer increases VAT, the electrician has no alternative but to pass on the amount of the VAT increase.) Otherwise, a quotation is a fixed price.

If you ask a gardener (or 'tree surgeon') to give you a price for uprooting a large tree you may get a different price. He may look at the tree, guess that its roots are relatively compact and say something like, 'I reckon I should get that all done in about four hours - maybe five; I charge £10 per hour.' That is an estimate; the price is not fixed - only the hourly rate. The gardener will do the job for you, at £10 per hour and it should take four to five hours - but if it takes six, you will have to pay £60. Clearly, it's always best to get a quotation.

And always check whether or not the price you've been given - fixed or estimated - includes VAT; it makes a big difference.

It's best too - though not essential, depending on the size of the job - to get either quotation or estimate in writing (I'd get a very dusty answer if I asked my hairdresser for a written quotation; anyway, the prices are displayed on the wall).

Beware cowboys

It is uncommon - not unheard of, just not a frequent occurrence - for a well-known local tradesman to do a job badly. As already remarked, word-of-mouth recommendation is much sought after by such service-providers.

But there are others. We've all heard of, or even experienced, the 'tarmac drive cowboys'. They '... just happen to be in the neighbourhood and have a couple of cube yards of black-top left over - we'll re-surface your drive really cheap, Guv'.' Avoid them... like the proverbial plague.

There may not be anything wrong with their materials - which may well be 'left over' from a nearby road construction job - but they seldom prepare an existing drive properly for re-surfacing. Nor will they always lay a sufficiently thick layer of new tarmac or asphalte. And, did you but know it, the price may not be all that cheap - even for the poor job they're doing. Too often the newly laid black-top peels off a month or so later. And what can you do about it? They don't give you their name and address, they don't have a firm's name on the side of their vehicle, they don't give you a proper bill or receipt... and always demand payment in cash ('Saves on the VAT, Guv'). A month later, you can't trace anyone to complain to; you're just stuck with having wasted your money.

The moral: don't have any work done on the spur of the moment by unidentifiable people or firms; get a firm price quotation -preferably from two or three people/firms and select the best - for a well-defined task to be done within a specified time. By doing that, you ensure that you will get what you pay for.

At a less-cowboy level, don't allow your decisions to be over-swayed by the promise of a, say ten-year, guarantee. Of what use is a guarantee from a firm that has gone out of business?

The goods

When the service you buy includes the provision and fitting of goods - eg, the bricks used in an extension, the wash-basin, etc installed in a refurbished bathroom... or the black-top used in a drive re-surfacing - then those goods are covered by the Sale of Goods Act, just as though you were to buy them directly. It is your right to expect and require them to be of satisfactory quality, fit for their purpose and 'as described'. If they are not, you can claim compensation - even if they are well installed.

Part-payments

When buying services - which often require work being undertaken over a period of time or a major investment in materials - you will sometimes be asked to pay a deposit or make a part payment. Avoid this whenever you can; but often it's unavoidable.

The least you can do is make sure you know the service provider's correct and full name and address - and make sure you get a formal receipt for the payment. Check whether the service-provider belongs to a trade association: many associations have schemes to protect consumers' pre-payments. Ideally, relate any advance payment to goods and material that have been delivered...onto your land.

Be careful about withholding instalment payments if you have a credit agreement. If you stop payments, your credit rating could be affected - which could cause trouble in the future.

Just as with goods from a mail order firm, as long as the total cost exceeds £100, there is an advantage in using your credit card when paying a deposit; if something goes wrong, you should have a joint claim against the credit card company for the full cost of the faulty service.

The other side of the payment coin is the service-provider's cash flow; you may have avoided paying instalments but it is then only reasonable that you do not delay paying the bill on completion.

With bigger jobs though - major house maintenance, extensions or improvements - and with mutual agreement, it is not unreasonable to withhold a small percentage of the total bill (say ten per cent) after completion for a (pre-agreed) month or so, in case anything needs to be made good.

They're not doing the job properly

With the purchase of services, potential sources of complaint are poor workmanship and slow (or non-) completion. You don't always have to wait until the job is complete to feel the need to complain. And it is right to act immediately.

If you believe a job is not progressing satisfactorily you should, at any stage, tell the service-provider of your dissatisfaction. Be specific: ongoing faults can often be corrected forthwith. Make a note of all in-progress complaints and criticisms, with the name of the person spoken to, the date and time, and their response; you may need this record to prove your case later.

(On the same track, keep a file of all relevant correspondence. But we go into more detail about writing complaint letters in Chapter 10. Take photographs too, of work you have complained about.)

If you are getting no satisfaction at all from your

defaulting service-provider in response to your complaints, you should think about having the work inspected by an independent person: another person in the same line of business is a good idea. Get a written report of the faults. You will of course have to pay for such a report, but if you end up in court (see Chapter 10) it will be invaluable - assuming it confirms your grounds for complaint.

Contracts

If the service you are purchasing is a relatively large one you may be expected to sign a 'standard' contract. If so, take your time and read it carefully before signing.

Some such contracts seek to limit the trader's responsibilities. This is *not* specifically illegal and may sometimes be valid in law. It all depends on whether it is unfair. If it is unfair, it has no legal force - but only a court can decide what is and is not unfair. It is never legal though to exclude liability for injury or death resulting from negligence in carrying out a service.

You, the consumer, are not bound by any standard term in a contract if it unfairly (that concept again) weighs the contract against you. Nor are you bound by any 'small print' that, for instance, gives the service-provider the right to vary the price without giving you the chance to withdraw from the contract. But these clauses are only potentially illegal if they are standard clauses; the same protection does not apply if you negotiate specific clauses of a like nature yourself.

But a contract is often to your advantage: it should spell out who does what, the exact nature of the work, the completion date and the fixed cost.

If you are offered a ready-made contract by a service-supplier (a builder, say), check that it covers the following points. If it doesn't add them in. And if you are preparing your own form of contract - which need be no more than an exchange of letters - ensure that it covers the same points:

- a detailed schedule of the work to be done, with breakdown of costs wherever possible.
- a clause to the effect that work not included in the agreed schedule and covered by the quotation (or estimate) should not be started without your authority (failing which, you are not bound to meet the cost so incurred).
- start and completion dates - perhaps including a penalty clause for late-completion if this is particularly important. (But penalties for late completion are hard to apply - there are so many good excuses.)
- the service-provider's responsibility for making good unavoidable damage to surrounding fabric (eg touching up paintwork damaged by fitting new doors, etc).
- a statement that the service provider clears up on completion.
- the service-provider's liability if serious damage is caused.

If you are dealing with a service-provider in the building or construction industry such clauses should present no problem: if your chosen service-provider doesn't want to sign up to them, go elsewhere. You're the boss. You're entitled to get what you pay for.

Off on your hols

You are entitled to get what you pay for on your holiday too. You are - usually - paying for fun in the sun, comfort and relaxation; you want a hassle-free break from the everyday work routine. Or you may want a bit of 'cul-cha' - a ramble round the ruins with a reputable guide: you still want comfort in the evenings and on 'rest days'. And you always want well-organised efficient travel and accommodation.

It is in the nature of tour operators' brochures to emphasise the best side of the holiday resort: if a hotel faces the beach but has an industrial estate at the back... the brochure photograph will show the hotel and the beach, not the factories. That's inevitable. But brochures must be truthful: if it's a two-mile walk along a dusty track to the beach they may not describe this as a few minute's pleasant stroll. Before booking your dream holiday:

- if the brochure is vague (and it often is, in some respect that concerns you particularly), ask specific questions. Clarify whatever is important to you:
  - distance to the sea? (In kilometres, not minutes walk)
  - is the beach free?
  - hotel room with a view...of what?
  - included meals?
  - babycare/babysitting facilities?
  - all, or which, excursions included in cost? (Extra costs?)
  - night flights? (Or possibility of last-minute flight-time changes?)
- try to find someone who has visited the resort recently and can tell you about it generally - and possibly about the hotel too.
- are there any hidden extras in the cost - or the possibility of price surcharges? (You ought to be notified of any surcharge no later than 30 days before your departure and it should not exceed 10 per cent; if more than 10 per cent, ABTA members must give you the right of cancellation with full refund.)
- is the price right - some operators offer free holidays for under-a-certain-age children - are you getting the best bargain?
- *read the small-print* in the contract - remember, you are signing a contract (with the tour operator, not the travel agent) and both you and the operator are legally bound by it. The booking conditions are part of the contract too. And

it's worth repeating: you're signing a contract...*read it carefully!*

Having taken all the reasonable precautions, you have rights if something goes wrong:

- it is a criminal offence for a brochure actually to mislead.
- paying by credit card offers you the same financial security as already mentioned, if the tour operator goes bankrupt or the holiday goes really wrong. (The holiday must cost at least £100 per person to qualify.)
- if your tour operator belongs to one of the trade associations (ABTA is the best-known) they will have a code of conduct to adhere to - this is not legally binding but is generally effective.
- you have a right to a 'reasonable' standard of accommodation -but beyond basic cleanliness, etc this depends on the standard you have paid for.
- holidays are now 'bonded' by the industry itself: that is, depending on the bonding organisation (ABTA, ATOL, etc), you should be able to finish your holiday and be flown back - even if the operator goes out of business.

If something is wrong when you are actually on holiday - room standard, food quality, beaches, excursions, guides, etc - tell the holiday company's local representative. Don't wait until you get back home to complain: many complaints can be sorted out on the spot. If they're not, it will improve your case back home if you made the complaint at the time too. And make a note of who you spoke to, when, where, and their response.

Luckily, most holidays work out well - or faults are corrected on the spot. But if something goes wrong, stays wrong and you can't get satisfaction from the operator on return, then ABTA operates an arbitration system which will endeavour to right wrongs amicably.

6

Doctors - Health-care - Lawyers - Estate agents

It's one thing arranging for a new conservatory to be built in the back garden...and tying the contractor down with agreements, completion dates, etc. It's quite another thing trying to lay down the law to a solicitor. Or a doctor... or even an estate agent.

Well not entirely. You still have rights - even when the person providing the service is sitting behind a large, impressive-looking desk and peering at you over the top of his glasses.

Let's look at various professional 'service-providers' one by one and see what you can expect... and what to do if something goes wrong.

Doctors

Most of us come into contact with doctors - 'our own' general practitioner (GP) and various specialists - through the National Health Service (NHS). Doctors themselves are registered with the General Medical Council (GMC), many are employed by or are under contract to the NHS. The British Medical Association (BMA) is their trade union. And beyond the GP, when hospitalisation or specialist care is needed, most of us still use NHS facilities.

General Practitioners

You have the right to choose which NHS GP you register with. (Or you can, of course, 'go private' - but most of us don't. There isn't a lot of advantage at GP level.)

If you are coming new to an area it would be wise to have a look at the local Health Centre (most NHS GPs operate in groups, from Health Centres - you can still choose your own individual doctor within the practice) or the GP's reception area; enquire about the appointment system (and the likely delays in being seen); see if you can have an informal pre-registration chat with one of the GPs - if not, perhaps with the Practice Manager (many practices now have a manager - to ease the doctors' administrative pressures); ask yourself whether you would feel comfortable consulting him or her (the doctor) if you were unwell. Ask around the neighbourhood for opinions on the practice generally and any doctors in particular. None of this investigation will help much in making a choice but at least you'll have done the best you can (and in many, particularly rural, areas, there is no realistic alternative to the local Health Centre practice. You choose the best of the predetermined bunch. And hope.).

Once registered, if you don't feel comfortable with the doctor or practice - no specific faults or complaints, just not what you want - you can change doctors; all you need to do is identify another doctor with whom you think you would feel more comfortable and ask to be transferred.

But an NHS GP is also within his rights to refuse to take you onto his list. And beware transferring from frying-pan to fire.

The health-care we want

Let's think now about what we want of our health-care service:

- we want to be - and stay - healthy
- we want our ailments speedily diagnosed and remedied - and injuries quickly set right
- we want specialist care when necessary

There is one major problem in deciding what to do if something goes wrong in our dealings with the NHS in general and GPs in particular: we do not have a contract with our doctor - we consumers are not paying our doctor for his/her services. There being no patient-doctor contract, NHS services are not subject to the Supply of Goods and Services Act.

But all is not lost: under common law everyone is under an obligation to take reasonable care not to injure anyone. Failure to take care is called negligence. A medical 'service-provider' must not be negligent - and can be sued if he/she is.

Other than in the courts, the general procedure for complaints about the NHS is not always clear. The Patients' Charter - copies of which are usually available in doctors' waiting rooms - now goes some way towards outlining and safeguarding our rights.

Complaining about health-care

Because the securing of our rights as health-care

consumers is still a somewhat entangled set of procedures it is most convenient to list them by 'reason' or complaint:

- if you feel there is something wrong with the (non-medical) way you are cared for, such as long delays in being seen, etc speak first to the doctor or to the practice manager; if you get no satisfaction there, complain to the Family Health Services Authority (FHSA).
- if you think that your GP has been negligent in a medical sense, such as incorrect diagnosis, incorrect treatment or delayed referral to a specialist, complain to the FHSA. Having complained to the FHSA, if still dissatisfied, you could refer your complaint on to the GMC. Or you could take the doctor to court for negligence. But proving medical negligence is far from straightforward. (You might have to prove, for instance, not merely that the treatment did no good, but that the condition was worsened as a direct result of the treatment. Or non-treatment.)
- if you have a complaint about your treatment - whether administrative or medical - in an NHS hospital, speak directly to the staff concerned first: many matters can be cleared up on the spot. If not, write to the hospital's complaints officer: they will want your name and hospital number, if possible the names of the staff involved, the date of the 'incident' and details of your complaint. Beyond this, for medical care matters, the Regional Medical Officer can, if appropriate, set up an independent professional review.

For most health-care complaints, including those about your GP, if you do not get satisfaction from the NHS authority, you can, having gone through the earlier stages, contact the Health Service Ombudsman. And, on a rather different aspect of health-care service:

- if you believe that your GP is guilty of professional misconduct, such as drunkenness, sexual relations with patients, or any other action likely to 'bring the profession into disrepute', write to the GMC giving full details and supporting evidence; if a Council member thinks there is a provable case, you will be required to make a sworn statement before the case is taken further within the GMC.

Of course, if you are a private patient, you are paying the doctor(s) and a contract therefore exists. You might be able to sue the doctor about the size of your bill. The same problems as outlined above, of proving medical negligence, will otherwise apply.

Lawyers

When we need a lawyer - which can mean either a solicitor or a barrister - our first point of contact will always be with a solicitor. (Barristers advocate in court; their professional services are only engaged by solicitors, never direct by Joe Public.)

If you are held by the police for questioning in a criminal case, you can have free legal aid, without any means test. Beyond this, all legal aid is means tested. But most of us law-abiding citizens will only require the services of solicitors for civil law matters or cases.

Legal aid is available for civil law cases - but it is severely means tested. The income level for free legal aid in civil law cases is set very low. Most people will find they have to pay part of the cost themselves: possibly as much as one-third of their disposable income (that is, total income less mortgage payments and similar commitments). Indeed, about half the population do not qualify for any (civil) legal aid at all.

Without doubt, one should not lightly resort to litigation. But there will always be some matters on which we need legal advice or help: buying or renting property, making a will, marital disputes, etc. In such cases you enter into a contract to buy the services of a lawyer. And the Supply of Goods and Services Act applies.

Hiring the solicitor

When engaging the services of a solicitor:

- arrange an initial 'pre-engagement' interview - to get 'the feel' of the solicitor and decide whether you will be happy to have them working for you.
- get details of the practice's hourly charges - for the solicitor in person and for the less-qualified staff who may do much of the background work.
- discuss in detail, how long your work is likely to take and thus, the likely bill - in other words, get an estimate. (It is often impossible to give an exact cost, but you and your solicitor should be clear about the 'ball-park' figures. You might wish to instruct the solicitor to check with you when the total cost is about to exceed a specified figure. At that point, you might discuss ways of keeping further costs down.)
- be as businesslike as possible yourself: make sure you fully understand what is going on; after a meeting confirm, in writing, anything agreed.

Dissatisfaction with your solicitor

If you are dissatisfied with your solicitor the legal profession has an excellent Solicitors Complaints Bureau (SCB) - set up in 1986 'to investigate impartially complaints made about solicitors.'

Before approaching the SCB with a complaint though, you should first contact your solicitor. All solicitors' offices operate an in-house complaints procedure - if in doubt about who to approach, write to the Senior Partner.

Set out your problem clearly and say how you think the problem can be resolved - eg a written apology, reduction in the bill, financial compensation. (If you are not sure whether you have grounds for complaint, the SCB operates a working-hours Helpline service - phone 01926 822007/8/9 - but they cannot give you legal advice as such.)

The SCB will look at complaints about:

- inadequate professional services (which includes, for instance, delays, lack of effective communication, etc) and
- professional misconduct (breach of confidentiality, etc)

It will not look at complaints of negligence, which may entail a court judgement, but it does have a panel of independent solicitors who, if consulted, will give one hour's free advice on whether they think a solicitor has been negligent and if so, what to do next. Apart from negligence cases, the SCB has the power to discipline a solicitor, to reduce a solicitor's bill in whole or in part and can order compensation of up to £1000.

There is also a Legal Services Ombudsman.

Estate agents

The first thing to accept in dealing with an estate agent is that their duty is to represent the house seller. Unlike doctors, lawyers, and various other professions, there is no compulsory qualification or registration for estate agents: anyone can set up shop as an estate agent. But there is a criminal law controlling their behaviour - the Estate Agents Act 1979.

The law requires that an estate agent advise a potential house-seller, in advance (orally or in writing):

- what their fees will be.
- how and when their fees will have to be paid. (Make sure that the fee is only paid when a sale is achieved, not merely on the introduction of a 'willing and able buyer'. Delete such clauses in any agreement before signing.)
- any personal interest they, or their associates may have in a property.

They must also arrange to hold any buyers' money - deposits, etc - on trust, in special accounts - and pay interest on such accounts containing £500 or more.

Choosing an estate agent

When you engage the services of an estate agent, you should:

- first get an idea of the charges and quality of service of a number of agencies before selecting one.
- decide whether to opt for a sole agency, a joint sole agency or a multiple agency. (A multiple agency choice will probably cost you more, even though you only pay a fee to the one who sells - a sole agency is probably the best choice.)
- if opting for a sole agency, put a time limit on the agreement so that, if the agency is not attracting buyers, you can take your business elsewhere. (You will need to give 14 days written notice of termination.)
- haggle over the costs with the agent. (Maybe don't pay for advertisements, which could reasonably be included in the commission; you may even be able to persuade the agent to cut their commission to get the business. It's worth a try if the market's slack.)
- never give 'sole selling rights' - which entitle an agent to claim a commission even if you sell the house privately.

As a buyer, the jungle is somewhat less regulated. You must be wary - all the time. There is one useful law though, the Property Misdescriptions Act of 1991. This requires property descriptions to be more accurate than was customary in the past: 'the truth, most of the truth, but not necessarily the whole truth'. They don't need to divulge everything unless asked, but if what they do tell you is innaccurate, they can be prosecuted.

Problems with estate agents

If something goes wrong in your dealings with an estate agent, your first recourse is to complain to the agency manager. If it is a chain-agency the next step would be to complain to the head office of the chain. If you believe the agency has contravened the law, get in touch with your local trading standards office. Otherwise, the next step is to contact the trade association, the National Association of Estate Agents; they operate a Code of Practice for their members. Unfortunately, both membership and compliance with the code are voluntary. And finally, there is an Estate Agents Ombudsman.

7

Water - Electricity - Gas
Telephone - The Post Office
Local government services

As well as the one-off services we buy - car servicing, a haircut, etc, - and the professions, of whose services we occasionally 'avail ourselves' - health-care, legal advice, etc - there are other services that we all take for granted. The supplying of water, gas, electricity, and a telephone connection are near-essential services. Utilities. We can't realistically do without them.

And although they are now profit-oriented rather than state-owned, they are still thought of as public services - of which we are all consumers, with rights. The Post Office, which is also a public service, is still state-owned - for now.

The real problem with the public services is not that they don't, on the whole, do their job well: it's more a question of knowing how to approach them, to right a wrong. They are such huge organisations that it's hard to get to grips with them.

In this chapter therefore we will look at each of the big utilities in turn, explore our entitlements, and signpost the appropriate route for complaints. This will usually take us into the ambit of the industry regulators.

Each of the utilities, but not the Post Office, has an industry watchdog or regulator - with the task, among others, of monitoring customer complaints; each of the utilities too has produced and published its own customers' Charter, which sets out your rights and the company's standards of service (phone your local utility company for a copy if you haven't got one).

Water

Water is supplied throughout Britain by a number of privately owned companies; each a regional monopoly. You have only to look at your annual water services account to see who the local supplier is.

The water company must connect your house to the water supply except in exceptional circumstances. They are entitled to levy a connection charge; they are also entitled to levy an infrastructure charge - which can be large. Although most consumers still pay a fixed annual sum for their water on the basis of the old house rating system, you can always ask for your water consumption to be measured by meter: the meter itself will usually be supplied free, but you will be charged for its installation. (£100 is a mid-range installation charge.) Most companies will pay compensation (usually £10) if the water supply is cut off for more than 24 hours.

If you have a complaint about your water supply,

approach the local company initially: look on your annual bill for advice on how to get a copy of their complaints procedure. If you can't decide who best to approach, write to the Customer Service Manager. Most complaints will be sorted out by the company itself. If you remain dissatisfied: write to the Director-General of Water Services at OFWAT about the actual service, or your bill; write to the Drinking Water Inspectorate about the quality of the water coming from your tap.

Electricity

Electricity is supplied throughout Britain by a number of regional monopolies; your local supplier sends you the bill each quarter. The reverse of the bill usually tells you who to approach with any complaint.

You are legally entitled to have your house connected to the electricity supplies - except in exceptional circumstances. They can charge the full cost of the connection; if you are moving into a house which has already been connected there will be no charge. The meter is part of the connection. All wiring on the house side of the meter is the householder's responsibility.

If you wish to complain about your electricity supply, start with the supply company. The contact person will usually be identified on the back of your quarterly bill. This will probably be the Customer Service Manager. If you are dissatisfied with the company's response to any complaint, write to the Director-General of Electricity Supply, the head of OFFER.

Gas

At the time of writing, the whole of Britain is supplied with gas by a single private company, British Gas. Inevitably, they have a number of regional offices: your regional office will be the one that sends you your quarterly gas bill. You have a right to be connected to the mains gas supply if your house is within 22.8 metres (25 yards) of the supply. British Gas will levy a standard charge for the connection; they may also ask for a deposit against future bills. If your house is beyond the 22.8 metre limit, British Gas may still connect you, at a price, but are under no obligation to do so. The gas meter is part of the installation.

If you need work doing on your in-house gas pipes and equipment, only a CORGI-registered gas fitter may do this. While the firms may be CORGI-registered, their employed fitters may not all be. Be sure to check this.

If you have cause to complain about your gas service, approach the local office initially (as on your bill). If they fail to satisfy you, write to the Gas Consumer Council. After that, if still dissatisfied, the Director-General of Gas Services at OFGAS.

Telephone

The major provider of telephone services throughout

Britain is the private company, BT - British Telecom. Other companies are busily encroaching on BT's operations though: cable TV companies are offering the use of their cables for telecommunications; Mercury, while using much of BT's line network, offers an alternative system; and there are several mobile phone networks. Nevertheless, at least for the forseeable future, BT is Britain's major telephone service provider.

You have a legal right to be connected to the BT telephone services, subject to satisfactory credit references; for a new connection there is a fixed charge (currently £116). If, having given BT seven days notice, you move into a house that is already connected to the telephone system and take over the existing line, there is no charge; if you don't give the necessary notice or don't take over the line within 24 hours, BT will charge you - currently £36.78.

You only need to have a BT connection socket; you don't have to rent (or buy) a BT phone, there is a vast assortment of approved phones (check for the circular green BT approval sign on the box or advert) on the market - and it's cheaper to buy your own than to rent.

If you have a complaint about the BT service... look on the back of your bill, or in the back of your directory ('The phone book') at the Code of Practice. In a nutshell: first phone 150; if still dissatisfied, phone that number again and ask for the Customer Service Manager; if you're still not satisfied, phone 0800 545458 for the Complaints Review Service. All these calls are free. (If you are a business phone user, call 0800 777 666 instead of 150 and 0800 555257 for the Complains Review Service.) If, after all that, you are still not happy, phone or write to OFTEL - but you should go through the earlier steps first.

The Post Office

The Post Office is still - so far - a nationalised undertaking. It operates as three separate businesses: Royal Mail (handling letters), Parcelforce (handling parcels) and Post Office Counter Services (handling the public - in post offices and sub-post offices).

Of greatest interest is of course Royal Mail. They have the exclusive right to deliver most mail in the UK. They set themselves targets for delivery of letters: to deliver First Class post on the next working day after collection, and Second Class post by the third working day after collection. Statistics show that they deliver more than nine out of ten First Class letters on time and do even better than that with Second Class. But they don't guarantee delivery times, other than for Special Delivery, Registered and Registered Plus letters - for any of which services you pay a few pounds more per item.

If you don't think your mail is getting through as well as it should, phone or write (Freepost) to your local Royal Mail Customer Service Centre (see the phone book). If dissatisfied with their response, contact your local Post Office Advisory Committee (POAC) or the Post Office Users' National Council (POUNC).

If you have any complaint about the other Post Office services, start with your local Head Postmaster - then move on to POAC or POUNC.

Local government services

The district or county council for the area in which you live is responsible for providing a whole range of services - from refuse collection to roads and footpaths, from libraries and museums to street sweeping.

Bearing in mind that any person or organisation providing a service has a duty of *care*, if you have a complaint against any local authority service-provider, the first step is to determine which council - district or county - is responsible. One way of finding this out is to check your annual council Tax demand notice or one of the accompanying leaflets. Or try the phone book. Failing that, start with your local District council: they will gladly re-direct you if a complaint is not for them.

Initially, approach the Director of the relevant council Department; if you fail to get satisfaction there, move up to the Chief Executive of the council. The next step, if still dissatisfied, is to approach your elected local councillor and/or the local press. The final step is to approach one of the Local Government Ombudsmen (there are three, each dealing with about a third of the country).

(The Ombudsmen deal only with matters of 'maladministration' though: where a council is too slow, breaks its promises, its own rules or the law, gives inaccurate information or reaches its decision in an incorrect way. They are not concerned with the relevant merits of a particular case - only that it should be properly dealt with.)

If you are moving into a brand-new house, its Council Tax band not having previously been assessed by the council, you can appeal against its band-assessment. Contact the Listing Officer at the council's Valuation Office. This facility is only open though, to first occupants of new houses.

8

Not just credit cards - Other forms of credit
A plus-point for credit buys - Your credit rating
Credit reference agencies

If you've the cash in your pocket - in 'readies' - or a comfortable balance in your bank account, you don't need to worry about money: once satisfied, you can immediately pay for anything you buy. And in many ways, that's the best way of going through life. You'll never be financially indebted to anyone. But until we win the Lottery, few of us are in that happy situation.

There are two other ways whereby we more ordinary mortals - maybe not poor, but not rich either - can buy what we want:

- the old-fashioned way - we can delay our purchase until we've saved up enough to pay for it, or
- today's way - we can buy it on credit and repay the loan, plus interest, thereafter (and thereby pay more for it).

Once again, the first way is the 'best'. But often we cannot delay a purchase... and nearly always we don't want to.

It also has to be said that a credit card, even if we pay off the full amount each month, is very convenient. There's no need to carry large amounts of cash about, nor prove our financial status when signing a cheque. For other than really major purchases - houses, cars, etc - our 'flexible friend' is all we need.

For major purchases, or if we don't (yet) have a credit card, most people can negotiate a loan or mortgage. This may be offered by the supplier of the major goods or services. But it pays to be cautious before agreeing to such a loan. (See below.)

Not just credit cards

The familiar credit cards are only one of several types of plastic cards which make our financial lives more convenient. There are:

- credit cards (eg Access, Visa) - permitting the card-holder to spend up to a specified limit, with flexible repayments (a fixed minimum amount - or more - per month) over a period of time: most charge an annual card-user fee plus a high rate of interest after a variable several-week interest-free period.
- debit cards (eg Switch, Delta) - given permission, a trader can debit the card-holder's bank account directly with the cost of a purchase. No credit involved.
- charge cards (eg American Express) - permitting the card-holder to spend up to a specified limit, the whole of which expenditure has then to be repaid on presentation of the monthly account: there is also an annual card-user fee. Credit for severely limited period only.
- company cards (as issued by major stores, eg Marks & Spencer) - permitting the card-holder to spend up to a

specified amount only in the issuing store, with repayments as for credit cards: no card-user fee but a high rate of interest after a variable several-week interest-free period.

- cheque guarantee cards (as issued by banks) - a customer's bank guarantees payment to a trader against a cheque (usually no more than £50) drawn in his/her presence: a glorified (but restricted) identification card. No credit involved.
- cash or service cards (as issued by banks and building societies) - a customer convenience, for withdrawing funds directly from one's own account, either when the bank is closed or to avoid queueing: the withdrawal amount is agreed and fixed. The card-user keys in a confidential Personal Identification Number (PIN) and obtains cash from a 'hole-in-the-wall' dispenser machine. No credit involved.

For greater user-convenience it is now common for banks, etc, to combine several of the above functions on a single plastic card. For example, my own (NatWest Bank) cheque guarantee card also serves as a cashcard and as a debit card (Switch). The Barclaycard credit card is also used as a Barclays Bank cheque guarantee card.

There are also so-called 'smart cards': an electronic system whereby a card is 'loaded' with a credit amount 'cashable' at participating traders. But these cards are not yet commonly available in the UK.

Other forms of credit

Credit cards and the like are not the only forms of credit available to consumers. Other forms of credit include:

- hire purchase - usually arranged by the trader selling the goods or services but financed by a separate finance company: for a specific item or service. (Note that under an HP agreement the goods are not yours until payment is complete: they can be repossessed - at seven days notice - if payments are in default.)

- bank or finance company personal loan - usually arranged by the consumer directly with a bank or finance company: not necessarily for a specific item or service. (Some loans are only given if *secured* on your home - see next item. Be wary of such loans.) An unsecured personal loan is often the most sensible form of credit.
- mortgage - usually arranged personally by the consumer, sometimes with the aid of an estate agent, with a bank or building society: usually *secured on* the property for which provided. (A secured loan means that if you fail to keep up the repayments, the lender can sell your home to cover his loss.)

Before agreeing to any credit arrangement, check the APR (which stands for Annual Percentage Rate of Charge). This has to be worked out in a standard manner by all lenders - with no scope for hidden extras - and is therefore the best way of comparing one credit deal with another.

A plus-point for credit buys

As already mentioned, in Chapter 3, the consumer has additional protection when buying a specific item on credit: the finance company - like the credit card company - is jointly liable for any claim the buyer may have against the trader. (This protection does not apply to a personal loan for an unspecified use.) A provision of The Consumer Credit Act of 1974, this protection is limited to purchases costing more than £100 and less than £30,000. Note that the protection is linked to the cost of the purchase, not to the amount of the loan.

Your credit rating

No one *has a right* to be given credit. Lenders have a right to decide for themselves whether or not to lend you their money. They don't have to explain why they refuse you credit - but they will usually give some indication of the reason. The most likely grounds on which credit would be refused are:

- you have an inadequate *credit score.* (Commercial lenders allot points for age, occupation, home-ownership, etc and add them up. Different lenders have different systems and different 'pass marks'. If one lender turns you down, you can always try another.)
- a credit reference agency has reported adversely on you and your credit history. (You are entitled to know the name and address of any credit reference agency consulted by a lender. Ask the lender within 28 days of their refusal, and they must tell you which agency within 7 days: if they didn't use an agency though, the lender doesn't have to reply to you. If you believe you have been wrongly refused credit, you are entitled to see - and seek to amend - your file at the credit reference agency: see procedure on page 80)

Under certain circumstances, if you sign up for a credit facility, you have the right to change your mind and cancel the deal. The conditions will be set out in the written credit agreement document. You can usually cancel if:

- the deal was very recent - within the last few days.
- the deal was agreed other than in the trader's business premises (which can include an exhibition stand) - eg at your home.
- the deal was made face-to-face - a deal agreed over the phone cannot be cancelled.

If, having signed up for a credit arrangement and, part way through repaying the loan, you come into money (the Lottery maybe?) it's nearly always a good idea to repay the loan. You will still, in total, have to pay more than the amount you originally borrowed; you have to compensate the lender for your use of his/her money during the on-loan period - and you will have to pay more than you expect. (Like a mortgage, much of the early repayments are often merely interest on the loan; it is only towards the end of a loan period that the capital repayment element increases significantly.) There may even be an early payment penalty. But the overall cost should still be cheaper than continuing to pay the instalments.

Credit reference agencies

There are, currently, four main credit reference agencies operating in the UK (see Help List). You have a right to a copy of an agency's file on you - and, if you think it's wrong, to seek to amend it. So either because you have been refused credit by one of the agencies, or just as a check:

- Write to the identified (or your selected, or to each) agency, giving your full name and address (including post code), and how long you have lived there; list any other addresses lived at in the last six years; and enclose a cheque or postal order for £1. (If you run your own business, give the business's name and address too. There may be another file.) Mention section 158(1) of the Consumer Credit Act 1974 and ask for a copy of your file.
- Within seven working days the agency must either send you your file, ask for more details to aid in identifying it, or tell you that it holds no information about you.

- The file, when you get it, will usually contain:
  - your name and address (from electoral roll)
  - other family members living in your household
  - other people at your address with a financial connection
  - a record of any court judgements for non-payment of debts
  - a record of any bankruptcies
  - details of other credit accounts (up-to-date or in arrears).
- Having seen the file you can ask for it to be amended if it contains incorrect information or information about people (including family members) with whom you do not, or no longer, have a financial connection. You cannot ask for correct details to be removed just because they are embarrassing.
- You are entitled to ask the agency to remove or change an incorrect entry. They must confirm within 28 days that they have or have not done so.
- If the agency does not remove or change the entry, you can, within a further 28-day period, send the agency *a notice of correction* to be added to your file. A notice of correction is a statement of 200 words or less, giving your side of the unchanged story. The statement should not be incorrect, defamatory, frivolous or scandalous or the agency can refuse to add it to your file. Once it amends your file or accepts your notice of correction, the agency must send details of the new file to any lender who has sought information about you in the previous six months.
- If the agency does not accept your notice of correction, it must refer the matter to the Director General of Fair Trading for a final decision; the Director General will invite you to comment. If you have not heard from the agency within 28 days of your sending a *notice of correction*, or if it refuses to accept it, you may yourself ask the Director General of Fair Trading to intervene.
- Phew! But it's important to ensure that your credit history is up-to-date and correct.

9

Employees' rights - Industrial tribunals
Further information

It's all very well having rights when you buy goods and services, but what about your own services: the work you do for your employer? Yes, employees too have their rights.

When you accept employment you enter into a contract - not necessarily written - with your employer. And where there is a contract, both parties have rights - and responsibilities. (Your rights as an employee - the terms and conditions of your employment - should be outlined in 'written particulars'. These should either be supplied to you within 13 weeks of starting work, or your attention directed to them, in a handbook or the like which is readily accessible to all employees.)

There are many laws concerning employment, and employees rights. This book is not the place to go into employment legislation as a whole. But let's look, briefly, at the big issues.

Employees' rights

As an employee you have, among other entitlements, the right:

- to be given due notice of dismissal (or non-renewal of a fixed-term contract):
  - one week's notice if you have worked for the employer for at least one month. (You do not have this right if you have not worked continuously for the employer for at least a month.)
  - two weeks' notice if you have worked for the employer continuously for two years plus an additional week's notice for each further continuous year (up to a maximum of twelve weeks).
  - twelve weeks notice if you have worked for the employer continuously for twelve years or more.
- not to be unfairly dismissed (or a fixed-term contract not renewed): that is, without notice, or by the employer refusing to allow a return to work after legal maternity leave. (You do not have this right unless you have completed two years continuous employment by the last day of your employment.)
- not to be 'constructively dismissed': that is, where the employer demonstrates an intention not to be bound by your contract. (Again, two years continuous employment is a necessary qualification for this right.)
- to receive, on request, a written statement of the reasons for dismissal (or non-renewal of a fixed-term contract). (Again, subject to two years continuous employment.)
- to be given paid time off work for ante-natal care and to return to work after

time off for pregnancy/confinement. (There is no qualifying period for ante-natal care but two years' continuous employment is a necessary qualification for the right to return.)

- to compensation payments if made redundant: and to a fair process of selection for redundancy. (Again, two years continuous employment is a necessary qualification.)
- when facing redundancy, to be given *reasonable* time off with pay to look for a new job, or to make arrangements for retraining: the *amount* of time off is unspecified - and will vary with individual circumstances. (Qualification: two years continuous employment working at least 16 hours per week; or five years if working 8 to 16 hours per week.)
- not to be discriminated against in employment on grounds of race, colour or ethnic origin, or sex or marital status - nor for trade union membership or activities.

Denied your rights?

If you think you've been denied your rights as an employee you can, usually, take your case to an industrial tribunal. But that should be the last resort. It is, of course, always best to try and sort the matter out with your employer first: merely reminding them of your rights may be sufficient for you to get them.

In any 'rights' negotiations with your employer it is nearly always best to enlist the aid of your trade union - that's assuming that you've had the sense to join the relevant union. (There's always strength in numbers.) Your fellow-employee union representative will usually have a good idea of your rights and how to go about achieving them; more importantly, the local rep can always call for help from union officers with vast experience in employment relations.

If your union can't persuade your employer to mend his/her ways - or if you've been trying unsuccessfully to negotiate alone - the next step in the complaints procedure is to contact the Advisory Conciliation and Arbitration Service (ACAS). ACAS, which is an independent service, separate from the industrial tribunal system, is there to help employees and employers resolve any dispute informally. The ACAS service is impartial, confidential and free; anything you say to an ACAS official cannot be revealed at a subsequent tribunal hearing without your permission.

Industrial tribunals

The last step in the full complaints process is for your complaint to be considered by an industrial tribunal. An industrial tribunal however, cannot hear matters relating to unpaid wages or to injuries at work due to the employer's negligence; in these cases you would have to take the employer to court under civil law.

There is a time limit on matters being referred to the tribunals: in most cases an application must be lodged (with the Central Office of the Industrial Tribunals) within three months of the event complained of. You must make absolutely sure that earlier attempts at resolving your complaints do not cause you to miss the deadline: you might be wise to apply while still going through the earlier stages; if the dispute is resolved the tribunal application can always be withdrawn.

Even if you haven't approached ACAS yourself before seeking an industrial tribunal hearing, details of your case will automatically be passed to them; ACAS will usually try to achieve a voluntary resolution.

An industrial tribunal hearing is like a court, but less formal. There will be a chairman (from the legal profession) and two lay members (one from a TUC panel, representing employees and one from a CBI panel, representing employers). As a complaining employee you can make your case alone, or be represented by a trade union officer (or a friend) or a lawyer; your employer may also be represented legally. Neither you nor the employer can have any financial assistance though; nor are costs normally awarded to either side. The tribunal's decision is final and usually given on the spot (and subsequently confirmed in writing). You may, for instance, achieve reinstatement or be awarded compensation.

Further information

There are many official booklets explaining different aspects of employment legislation. The subjects range from unfair dismissal to time off entitlements - as provided by the Employment Protection (Consolidation) Act 1978 (amended by the Employment Act 1989). There are many laws relating to employment conditions and rights: you need all the explanatory advice you can get. The leaflets are free: ask at your local Job Centre (unsurprisingly, one of the more 'popular' booklets is entitled *Unfairly Dismissed?* numbered PL 712 (REV 10)).

There is also a booklet (*Industrial Tribunal Procedures* - ITL 1) explaining how to apply, what to do, what to expect, etc. This too can be obtained from your local Job Centre or direct from the Central Office of the Industrial Tribunals.

10

How to complain
Unsatisfactory private sector service
Where to get help
Complaints about professional and public services
The last resort - in court

We have now looked at many of the rights to which you, as consumer, are entitled. We have looked too at ways of avoiding the need for you to exercise those rights: prevention always being the best cure. But occasionally something will go wrong; Murphy's Law doesn't exist for no reason. And when something does go wrong, when you *don't* get what you pay for, you have to *complain*.

One small step...

It's always best to start by explaining what's wrong, in person, face to face. Take your over-stretched-fit pullover, your inoperative walkman, your book with missing pages, your incorrect paint back to the shop you bought it from and tell a shop assistant - preferably the one who sold it to you. Do this as soon as possible. Go into the store you bought your new TV set from and explain to the sales person that the picture's fuzzy - or whatever. If you can't get to the store quickly, phone them.

Often, you will get a new, working, walkman or a fully-paged book straight away, in exchange. And this may well be what you want.

If the pullover is unwearable though, you won't want another one the same. You may be content with a credit note and will happily select a different item of clothing of like value in the same shop. But swimming trunks won't keep you as warm as a pullover (and be wary: once you accept a credit note, if you can't find anything else you want, you may not later be able to swap it for cash).

You may prefer a cash refund straight away - so that you can shop around for an acceptable comfortable-fit pullover. Many times too, you will get this refund without question. You should: it's your right.

If the assistant has no authority to put right your faulty purchase - or simply refuses - speak to the supervisor or the store manager.

It helps to have with you, when you register a complaint, your receipt or other proof of purchase - a credit card slip, a cheque stub even. If the defective goods are small, you should obviously bring them with you too. You do not though, have to arrange for a faulty TV, fridge or three-piece suite to be brought back to the store: the seller must arrange to collect - at his expense.

If the shop is sympathetic and willing, but your faulty goods cannot be replaced on the spot, you should *agree* a date by which they will provide a satisfactory replacement.

Play it cool

When dissatisfied, it is important that you explain what is wrong - and what you want (replacement, repair, refund, whatever) - clearly, calmly and politely. Even if the staff are thoroughly unhelpful and obstructive, stay cool.

Hear what they say, tell them you are not satisfied, and do not accept their offer or refusal; tell them that you will be taking the matter further. If it's a chain-store and you've got up as far as the local manager - say that you will certainly be writing to their head office. In any case, say that you will have to consider taking legal action for compensation. (See below for how to do this - it's not too difficult.)

Before you leave the shop, still not satisfied, make a note of the date and time, the names of those to whom you spoke and, as near as possible, what they said.

Unsatisfactory private sector service

Take much the same line with a complaint about an unsatisfactory service. If your car comes out of an annual maintenance service sounding rougher than when you took it in: complain. If your replacement windows let in the rain, or won't open: complain. Point out the faults calmly and politely: don't lose your cool.

If your complaint is that the price is excessive - and you didn't agree a price in advance - you're on a sticky wicket. If, because of dissatisfaction with the workmanship, you haven't yet paid the full (agreed) price of whatever you've had done, think about withholding further payments: but read the small print on any contract you've signed. It might be wise to take legal advice before withholding payment.

If you are paying through any sort of credit agreement - perhaps paying monthly instalments to a finance company which has paid, or will pay the service-provider in full when the money is due - it is usually unwise to withhold payments. The finance company is not at fault; you may harm your credit rating (see Chapter 8) and deter future lenders.

As with faulty goods, if you get nowhere with your complaint to the service-provider, tell them you are notsatisfied and will be taking the matter further. (Either with their head office and/or possibly in the courts.) And as before, make a note of time, date, persons spoken to, and their response.

Put it in writing

Having reported your complaint in person and, in this case without success, the next step is to put it in writing. Having told the shop-keeper or service-provider that you would be taking the matter further, it is best, initially, to repeat your complaint in writing, to them.

At this stage you will often find it useful to contact your local Citizens Advice Bureau. They can help you with the rest of the process - perhaps even expand on, or update the advice in this book.

Write to the shop-keeper, service-provider boss, or store manager - the latter even if you didn't get that high up when complaining in person. If you don't already know it, phone the firm and ask the telephone operator the name of the person you want to write to: it's always best to address someone personally. Make sure the letter is polite and business-like.

In your letter, give all the necessary facts, stating:

- the particular item or service you are complaining about.

- when (and where) you bought the item or ordered (and received) the service, and the price you were quoted or charged. (If possible, enclose photocopies -*not* originals - of relevant bills, receipts, guarantees, etc.)
- whenever possible, the names and positions of those who have been involved - both initially and when you later complained - in the transactions and discussions.
- what, in your view, is wrong with the item or service. (You may not know what is wrong with, say, an inadequate vehicle maintenance service - but you can always list the symptoms.)
- what you want done to remedy the situation: eg a replacement, repair, or refund, or the job redone.
- a date by which you expect a satisfactory response - be reasonable, allow them a couple of weeks perhaps.

In most cases, where you are on firm ground with your complaint, and reasonable - ie, within your rights - in your request, the formal letter will suffice; just before the deadline you will often receive a reply agreeing to your remedies. If not, within a day or so after the deadline, write to them again, advising that you are now, within seven days, going to seek compensation in the courts. This again will sometimes provoke a cave-in.

With anything other than the most minor complaint, you should post such letters by Recorded Delivery - and ask for the proof of delivery. And always, keep a copy of everything you send (and receive).

Expert opinions

At this stage, particularly with faulty or over-priced services - which may be a matter of judgement - it will often be worth your while seeking an expert opinion, in writing. The 'expert' need be no more than another (reputable) roof-tiling firm or garage or whatever; their opinion will be just as valid as that of the one about whom you are complaining. With a thought-to-be faulty car maintenance service, consider asking one of the motoring organisations to inspect and comment. (You will almost certainly have to pay for any of these opinions... but they could help you prove your case in court.)

It is also often worth taking photographs of whatever it is you are complaining about.

Assistance from elsewhere

You might also, at this pre-court stage, seek assistance in your fight to *get what you pay for*, from a relevant trade association. Many trade associations have Codes of Practice; unfortunately, they can seldom enforce these recommendations upon recalcitrant association members. But they can 'lean on' the association members about whom you are complaining. This will often suffice.

Similarly, although faulty goods are legally the responsibility of the trade who sold them to you, you might find it helpful to approach the manufacturer for support. Manufacturers have the ability to stop supplying a trader with their goods if he/she is reneging on a responsibility. It is also useful to remind a manufacturer of any guarantee they issue.

With both trade associations and manufacturers, the earlier 'play it cool' advice is equally relevant. Straightforward factual letters incorporating a polite request for assistance are the best approach and will often pay off.

Complaints about professional and public services

If you have a complaint about a professional service-provider, or one of the public services, the procedures will be much the same; talk to someone about your complaint first - by phone or by visiting an office. Thereafter, confirm it in writing, giving all the facts and details.

It is after that first written complaint that there may be differences when dealing with professional and public services. Most next-level complaint addressees have been identified in earlier chapters. Some complaint processes may require you to fill in an official-looking form rather than writing a further letter. This is no more difficult than a letter - easier, perhaps - and you will be advised how to get the appropriate form. (Again, if you find the form difficult, your local Citizens Advice Bureau may be able to help.)

Once you've progressed through the multi-level official complaint procedures it will seldom be necessary - or possible - to contemplate legal action. You'll have done all you can.

The last resort

With private sector suppliers of faulty goods or services it *will* sometimes be necessary - and appropriate - to take them to court. This should be the last resort though. Anyone can claim compensation through the civil courts.

Although to be avoided if at all possible, it is not difficult - if a 'small claim'. A small claim is a claim for payment of not more than £3,000; the claim is made through a county court by a simple and informal procedure.

You can make a claim in respect of a debt, bad

workmanship, an accident, supply of faulty goods, non-supply of goods, or the repayment of a loan. The purpose of a small claim is to achieve financial compensation.

The court will charge you a fee in respect of your claim; this fee is added to the amount you are claiming from the trader or service-provider. If your claim is successful it costs you nothing. It is wise to think before starting a claim though: if the person from whom you are claiming has no money, going through the court procedure won't help. But this would be an unusual situation with an established trader.

In most cases you should not need legal assistance. The court will give you the appropriate forms and tell you what to do. And if necessary, a Citizens Advice Bureau should help you fill in the forms.

The summons form

You start the claim procedure by contacting your nearest county court; you need (at least) three copies of the claim form N1 - Default Summons Form; when you return the forms you have to pay the court fee (basically ten per cent of the amount claimed, but with minimum and maximum cut-off limits). The three copies are to provide:

- one for you - the *Plaintiff*
- one for the court; and
- one for the court to send to the person you are claiming from - the *Defendant*. (You will need extra copies of the form if your claim is against more than one person: one each.)

The N1 forms are genuinely simple and straightforward. As a consumer you will usually be claiming on your own behalf - you give your full name and address. If you are making the claim as a trader yourself you need to provide name, address, and trading nature (limited company, 'trading as', etc) of the business. You also have to give details of the defendant: person's name (full if known, otherwise initials) and address if an individual, firm's name and details if not.

You then have to give a brief (one- or two-line) description of the claim, plus a more detailed outline of the particulars. Keep the detailed particulars as concise as possible: stick to the facts and list them in sequence, preferably in numbered paragraphs. Include:

- the terms of the original contract - anything from the bill or receipt to the relevant clause(s) in a longer (attached) document.
- the specific complaint - don't elaborate, just say what's wrong.
- the remedy you are seeking - refund, repair costs, etc.

The court will send a copy of the summons form to the defendant who has 14 days from the date the summons is delivered in which to respond. It's up to you to make sure that the defendant's name and address are correct: if the summons isn't delivered you will be told - and must try again to determine the correct address. (Until delivery is made, there's no case.)

When the defendant receives the summons he/she will either agree the claim and pay you; or meet you in court and argue their defence.

Be warned: if the defendant decides to contest the case, it is likely to be transferred from your county court to one that is preferred by the defendant. You will then have to attend that court to plead your case - and you will have to meet your own expenses in getting there. If your claim is small, ask yourself if it's worth a long journey.

The case

A small claims case is heard by a District Judge, in private, in chambers; only the plaintiff and the defendant are present (plus any associates or witnesses called by either party).

The big advantages of the small claims court are its informality (designed to obviate the need for legal assistance), the judge's role as an investigative arbitrator, and the absence of legal charges (even if you lose your case you will not be liable for the other party's costs - unless you fail to turn up for the hearing or, exceptionally, the court decides that your claim is totally unreasonable and a waste of the court's time).

If the case is found in your favour the defendant will usually pay you, through the court. If not, you will need to decide whether it is worth further legal action, which may be costly. You may well now need to consult a solicitor. And we're outside the scope of this elementary book. Most times though, the system works before reaching this final stage.

So far, throughout this little book, we have talked mainly about the national organisations that can help you, as a consumer, to get what you pay for. There are many branches of these organisation, or local offices, local to you. Consult your telephone directory (the phone book) for nearby help: there's a lot there, just at the end of a phone line. But again, you may need to seek the help of the national organisations direct. In this chapter are suggestions for who to look out for locally (in the phone book under...) and addresses and phone numbers for national organisations.

Many of the national organisations will provide you with free leaflets or booklets explaining exactly how to make a complaint. The Office of Fair Trading particularly issues a number of Know Your Rights booklets; these booklets are also usually available from the Trading Standards Department of your county council.

Local advice and support

- **Citizens Advice Bureaux**
  Look in the phone book under **Citizens**... (there'll be one in your nearest town)
- **Environmental health officers**
  (Food purchase and restaurant quality complaints): look for **Environmental Services - Health** (or **Food**) in the phone book under your **District Council**
- **Family Health Services Authority**
  (Complaints about NHS treatment): look in the phone book under **Family**...
- **Job Centres**
  (For advice and leaflets on employees' rights: look in the phone book under **Employment Service** for the nearest of many
- **Small claims courts**
  (All small claims start - and usually finish - in a county court): look for **County Courts** in the phone book under **Courts**
- **Trading Standards Offices**
  Look for the **Trading Standards Department** in the phone book under your **County Council** (there will be several local offices in each county)
- **Weights and Measures Department**
  (For short weight/measure complaints): usually part of the county council's Trading Standards Department (see above)

Trade and professional associations

- **AA** (The Automobile Association)
  Technical Information Unit, Lambert House, Stockport Road, Cheadle, Cheshire SK8 2DY
- **ABTA** (Association of British Travel Agents)
  55-57 Newman Street, London W1P 4AH. **Tel** 0171 637 2444

- **CORGI** (The Confederation for the Registration of Gas Installers)
  4 Elmwood, Chineham Business Park, Basingstoke, Hants RG24 8WG. **Tel** 01256 708133
- **Electrical Appliances, Association of Manufacturers of Domestic**
  Rapier House, 40-46 Lambs Conduit Street, London WC1N 3NW. **Tel** 0171 405 0666
- **Estate Agents, The National Association of**
  Arbon House, 21 Jury Street, Warwick CV34 4EH
  Tel 01926 496800
- **GMC** (General Medical Council)
  44 Hallam Street, London W1N 6AE. **Tel** 0171 580 7642
- **Mailing Preference Service**
  Freepost 22, London W1E 7EZ. **Tel** 0171 738 1625
- **Mail Order Publishers, Association of**
  1 New Burlington Street, London W1X 1FD
  Tel 0171 437 0706
- **MOPS** (Mail Order Protection Scheme)
  16 Tooks Court, London EC4A 1LB. **Tel** 0171 405 6806
  (But contact relevant magazine or newspaper's advertising manager or complaints department first)
- **MOTA** (Mail Order Traders Association)
  100 Old Hall Street, Liverpool L3 9TD. **Tel** 0151 227 4181
- **Motor Manufacturers and Traders Ltd, Society of**
  Forbes House, Halkin Street, London SW1X 7DS
  Tel 0171 235 7000
- **RAC** (The Royal Automobile Club)
  P O Box 100, RAC House, Bartlett Street, South Croydon, Surrey CR2 6XW. **Tel** 0181 686 0088
- **Radio, Electrical and Television Rétailers' Association Ltd**
  RETRA House, St John's Terrace, 1 Ampthill Street, Bedford MK42 9EY. **Tel** 01234 268110
- **Solicitors Complaints Bureau**
  Victoria Court, 8 Dormer Place, Leamington Spa, Warwickshire CV32 5AE. **Tel** 01926 820082/3 **Helpline Tel** 01926 822007/8/9 (during working hours only)

National organisations

- **Advertising Standards Authority**
  2-16 Torrington Place, London WC1E 7HN. **Tel** 0171 580 5555
- **Citizens Advice Bureaux, National Association of**
  (But see the phone book for your nearest Bureau for help.)
  Myddelton House, 115-123 Pentonville Road, London N1 9LZ. **Tel** 0171 833 2181
- **Consumers Association**
  (*Which?* magazine) 2 Marylebone Road, London NW1 4DF
  Tel 0171 486 5544
- **Drinking Water Inspectorate**
  Department of the Environment, Romney House, 43 Marsham Street, London SW1P 3PY. **Tel** 0171 276 0900
- **Gas Consumers Council**
  6th Floor, Abford House, 15 Wilton Road, London SW1V 1LT. **Tel** 0171 931 0977
- **National Consumer Council**
  20 Grosvenor Gardens, London SW1W 0DH
  Tel 0171 730 3469
- **Office of Fair Trading** (OFT)
  15-25 Bream's Buildings, London EC4A 1PR
  Tel 0171 242 2858
  OFT Consumer Helpline Tel 0345 224499 - local call rate)
  ...and for supply of the free OFT leaflets:
  OFT Publications
  PO Box 2, Central Way, Feltham, Middx TW14 0TG
  Tel 0181 398 3405

Industry regulators

- **OFFER** (Office of Electricity Regulation)
  Hagley House, Hagley Road, Birmingham B16 8QG
  Tel 0121 456 2100

- **OFGAS** (Office of Gas Supply)
  Stockley House, 130 Wilton Road, London SW1V 1LQ
  Tel 0171 828 0898
- **OFTEL** (Office of Telecommunications)
  50 Ludgate Hill, London EC4M 7JJ. **Tel** 0171 634 8700
- **OFWAT** (Office of Water Services)
  Centre City Tower, 7 Hill Street, Birmingham B5 4UA
  Tel 0121 625 1300
- **POUNC** (Post Office Users' National Council)
  England: 6 Hercules Road, London SE1 7DN
  Tel 0171 928 9458
  Northern Ireland: 7th Floor, Chamber of Commerce House, 22 Great Victoria Street, Belfast BT2 7PU
  Tel 01232 244113
  Scotland: 2 Greenside Lane, Edinburgh EH1 3AH
  Tel 0131 244 5576
  Wales: 1st Floor, Caradog House, St Andrews Place, Cardiff CF1 3BE. **Tel** 01222 374028

Ombudsmen

- **Banking Ombudsman**
  70 Grays Inn Road, London WC1X 8NB. **Tel** 0171 404 9944
- **Building Societies Ombudsmen**
  Millbank Tower, Millbank, London SW1P 4XJ
  Tel 0171 931 0044
- **Estate Agents Ombudsman**
  Beckett House, 4 Bridge Street, Salisbury SP1 2LX
  Tel 01722 333306
- **Health Service Ombudsman**
  Millbank Tower, Millbank, London SW1P 4QP
  Tel 0171 217 4051
- **Legal Services Ombudsman**
  22 Oxford Court, Oxford Street, Manchester M2 3WQ
  Tel 0161 236 9532

- **Local Government Ombudsmen**
  London and the South-East: 21 Queen Anne's Gate, London SW1H 9BU. **Tel** 0171 915 3210;
  South-West and Central England and East Anglia: The Oaks No 2, Westwood Way, Westwood Business Park, Coventry CV4 8JB. **Tel** 01203 695902;
  North England: Beverley House, 17 Shipton Road, York YO3 6FZ. **Tel** 01904 663200
- **Parliamentary Commissioner for Administration** (the Central Government Ombudsman)
  Church House, Great Smith Street, London SW1P 3BU
  Tel 0171 276 3000

Credit reference agencies

- **CCN Credit Systems**
  Consumer Affairs Department, PO Box 40, Nottingham NG7 2SS
- **Credit Data and Marketing Services**
  CCA Department, Dove Mill, Dean Church Lane, Bolton, Lancs BL3 4ET
- **Equifax Europe (UK)**
  Ltd Consumer Affairs Department, Spectrum House, 1A North Avenue, Clydebank, Glasgow G81 2DR
- **Infolink Ltd**
  CCA Department, Regency House, 38 Whitworth Street, Manchester M60 1QH

Employment organisations

- **ACAS** (Advisory Conciliation and Arbitration Service)
  Head office: 27 Wilton Street, London SW1X 7AZ
  Tel 0171 210 3000. There are also regional offices throughout

the country - see the phone book, under Advisory...

☼ **Industrial Tribunals**
Central Office of the, Southgate Street, Bury St Edmunds, Suffolk IP33 2AQ. **Tel** 01284 762300

Index

INDEX

INDEX

Also Published by

Need2Know

Safe as Houses

Security and Safety in the Home

Gordon Wells

ISBN 1 86144-013-8

£5.99 100pp Pub July 96

650,000 burglaries take place in the UK each year; this is an average of 1 in every 49 seconds.

5,000 fatal accidents occur in the home in the UK every year.

With these statistics, everyone should be aware of the dangers and do everything possible to increase security and safety in the home.

Buying a House

Ease the Path to your New Front Door

John Docker

ISBN 1 86144-004-9

£5.99 148pp Pub Jan 96

Many people have been put off home buying in recent years, whether buying for the first time or making a move. *Buying a House* aims to make the purchase of a house an exciting and rewarding achievement.

16.5 million are aged between 15 and 34 years and are the house buyers of the future.

Need2Know Series

For further details and to order further copies, please contact

Kerrie Pateman (Editorial)
Pat Wilson (Marketing)
Need2Know
1-2 Wainman Road
Woodston
Peterborough
Cambs
PE2 7BU

Tel 01733 390801
Fax 01733 230751

Need2Know are always interested in proposals for new titles. Please contact the above address for information and brief.

____ **Travel Without Tears**..£5.99

____ **Prime Time Mothers**...£5.99

____ **Parenting Teenagers**..£5.99

____ **Planning Your Wedding**.....................................£5.99

____ **Coping With Bereavement**...................................£5.99

____ **The Facts About The Menopause** **New Edition**......£6.99

____ **Make The Most Of Family Life**............................£4.99

____ **Take A Career Break**..£4.99

____ **Stress-Busting**...£5.99

____ **Subfertility**...£6.99

____ **A Parent's Guide To Drugs**.................................£6.99

____ **A Parent's Guide To Dyslexia And Other Learning Difficulties**..£6.99

____ **Starting School**...£6.99

____ **Education Matters**..£6.99